WHAT ARE PEOPLE SAYING ABOUT THIS BOOK?

"General Wyche's book tells an inspiring story of triumph from very humble beginnings, rising from private to three-star general in the US Army. Along the way, he evolved deep and compelling insights on leadership that will greatly benefit any reader.

General Wyche is a true supply chain professional who managed a massive $58 billion global support operation for the US Army. He identifies six traits that mark the very best logisticians. He points out that supply chain professionals must manage the supply chain from an end-to-end perspective. As he says, "We must always see ourselves end-to-end." Although these lessons of leadership are often told in a logistics setting, they are equally valuable to anyone seeking to lead people on a journey to excellence.

General Wyche recommends a hands-on leadership style, grounded in a deep connection with people in the organization. He shows how real leadership means truly connecting with people in a very visible manner.

This book is packed with practical advice that the reader can use today, and stays away from vague principles of little direct value. For example, General Wyche provides deep insights into the planning process. After discussing planning principles, he notes that, "No matter what the size of the problem, the process stays the same." He also provides eight steps for effective training. And he offers insightful advice for managing "up" in an organization. In addition, he discusses best practices for organizing a supply network that are directly applicable to commercial enterprises. He further advises the reader on how to mitigate the real and growing cyber-security threat, something everyone faces.

The book concludes with invaluable guidance on becoming a great leader. His "mirror test" includes ten questions that aspiring leaders would want to ask themselves, with the final question being the most compelling: "Would I want to work for me?"

This book is an extremely useful guide for all supply chain professionals and indeed any leader, and is filled with practical advice that the reader can immediately apply.

General Wyche has been an invaluable member and participant in the Global Supply Chain Institute Advisory Board at the University of Tennessee."

Review/Endorsement by the Global Supply Chain Institute at the University of Tennessee:

Ted Stank, PhD, The Harry J. and Vivienne R. Bruce Chair of Excellence in Business and Professor of Supply Chain Management at the University of Tennessee

Shay Scott, PhD, Executive Director of the Global Supply Chain Institute and Distinguished Lecturer at the University of Tennessee

Paul Dittmann, PhD, Assistant Department Head and Senior Lecturer at the University of Tennessee

"In the time that I have known General Larry Wyche, I have been impressed with his life's mission to be a strong leader with a servant's heart. His Christian foundation has served him well while being a good steward with opportunities that he created through hard work and determination. General Wyche's journey from humble beginnings to Lieutenant General in the Army demonstrates that his unwavering determination and talents of leadership have been an inspiration to everyone he has had the opportunity to work with. Larry is a clear example of how to succeed in life by helping the people you work with to succeed. Even after retiring from the Army, General Wyche continues to use his leadership skills to inspire and help others working on world changing projects. It is an honor to be his friend."

Michael C. Riddle Jr., MD
Co-Owner, The Riddle Institute for Regenerative Medicine

"Larry Wyche has done a better job capturing the spirit of servant leadership in this book than any other author I know. *Shirts Off Our Backs, Boots Off Our Feet* is this decade's "Lean In" for committed leaders of all genders, paths, and purposes. I wish I had read this book years ago—it restores my faith in so many ways, faith in leaders, faith in our military, faith in humanity. Any leader will be uplifted, and find themselves in a better place, having read *Shirts Off Our Backs, Boots Off Our Feet*."

Thomas A. Kolditz, PhD
Director, Doerr Institute for New Leaders, Rice University
Author, *In Extremis Leadership: Leading As If Your Life Depended On It*

"LTG(R) Larry Wyche possesses a rare combination of mastering his craft, the science of logistics and supply chain, the art of leadership and the passion to serve our nation. I would trust him to take my son to war. I can think of no higher compliment from one soldier to another. He is the best leader I know. Larry Wyche's book is the best logistics and leadership military book of its kind—every Soldier, sailor, airman, and Marine should have this book as their core leadership resource."

SGM(R) Tom Stiefermann

"LTG(R) Larry Wyche's life is an American success story in his professional as well as personal life. In this book, he captures the tools/techniques he applied; but more importantly the leadership style he employed to be effective and highly successful. I worked with Larry seven years in the field and two in the pentagon—learned from him daily and saw first hand a strong, caring, smart leader who took care of soldiers."

General Benjamin Griffin
Former Army Materiel Commander

SHIRTS OFF OUR BACKS

BOOTS OFF OUR FEET

Lieutenant General Larry Wyche
(U.S. Army, Retired)
with Jeff Jurgensen

emerge

24 23 22 21 20 19   8 7 6 5 4 3 2 1

SHIRTS OFF OUR BACKS BOOTS OFF OUR FEET – How Leadership Enables Logistics and Supply Chain Execution and Gives You the Edge to Win.

TULSA, OKLAHOMA

Published by:
Emerge Publishing, LLC
9521B Riverside Parkway, Suite 243 Tulsa, Oklahoma 74137
Phone: 888.407.4447 www.EmergePublishing.com

Library of Congress Cataloging-in-Publication Data:

ISBN: 978-1-949758-36-8 Paperback
ISBN: 978-1-949758-37-5 Digital/E-book

BISAC Category:
BUS087000 BUSINESS & ECONOMICS / Production & Operations Management
BUS063000 BUSINESS & ECONOMICS / Strategic Planning
BUS020000 BUSINESS & ECONOMICS / Development / Business Development

TABLE OF CONTENTS

DEDICATION

This book is dedicated to my wife and best friend,
Denise for her unwavering support and sacrifice and my
children, David, Tori and Meagan. Also, a special thank you to
the soldiers, civilians, logisticians and supply chain professionals
I've had the privilege, opportunity and honor to serve with
over the last 42 years.

Over the years private, cadet and Lieutenant General with wife, Denise.

FOREWORD
by Drayton McLane

I met Larry nine years ago when I was the owner of the Houston Astros. He threw out the first pitch at Minute Maid Park for an Astros and Pittsburgh Pirates ball game. He threw an impressive strike. I told him he was in the wrong profession and we should think about signing him to the Astros.

At that time he was a Brigadier General and had a very successful Army career behind him. However, as it turned out, he was just getting started. Larry served another nine years and rose to the rank of Lieutenant General – and not just because he could throw a pretty decent fast ball. His contribution to our country culminated in Larry serving as the second in command of the Army Materiel Command, a global enterprise with tens of thousands of Soldiers, Army civilians and industry employees. Larry made a big impression on me the day we met. He also gave me a real appreciation of the selfless service and sacrifices that he - and so many others had made as Soldiers.

From humble beginnings, what Larry has accomplished is astonishing, impressive and inspirational. Rising through the ranks from Private to Sergeant to Lieutenant General, he has *"been there and done that"* as they say in the military *(so I'm told)*.

I've read that General Eric Shinseki, the 34th Chief of Staff of the Army, would often say "soldiering is an affair of the heart". This is certainly true of Larry as a Soldier, logistician and supply chain professional. Supporting soldiers is an obsession with Larry. In his line of work, a misstep could mean lives were lost. Today, he carries that same passion for customer support in the civilian world.

All who served with Larry Wyche know he'd give the shirt off his back or boots off his feet so a Soldier could carry on with their mission. Larry truly believed and lived this vision - day in and day out.

I've met some great leaders and great players in my time; Larry is a true leader and a real game-changer. He has a God-given talent to motivate and inspire, while always remaining humble and approachable.

In this book, Larry shares the stories, experiences, and lessons from a lifetime in uniform. Whether you're a young Soldier, an experienced military leader, or a logistics and supply-chain professional in the civilian world, Larry's story has something for you. In about the time it takes to fly from Houston to Los Angeles for a business meeting (or a Dodgers game), you can read Larry's words, learn the lessons he did, and improve yourself and your logistics team. I encourage you to do it. No matter what kind of business you're in – we need more leaders willing to give the *Shirts off their back and Boots off their feet!*'

Drayton McLane
Former Owner-Houston Astros Baseball Team

INTRODUCTION

In 1968, when I was 10 years old, I lived and worked with my grandmother and grandfather in Pleasant Shade, Virginia, which is about five miles west of a town called Emporia. Back then, Pleasant Shade's population was about 1,000 and Emporia's around 5,300. To show how little things change in that part of the country, today, over fifty years later, Emporia's population is still only 5,900.

During that time, I stayed with my grandparents, because my Mom and Dad had moved north to New Jersey to find better jobs. Even though my parents weren't in Emporia, they were still very involved in our lives.

My grandparents were sharecroppers. Good, honest people. But money did not come easy to them. For me and my siblings, money did not come at all. Although I remember thinking my life was pretty good, even at that age I knew it was also pretty hard.

My grandparents worked in the tobacco fields. During the summer, temperatures rose well above 90 degrees, and at midday in Virginia, the humidity felt like a relentless weight on my back. Summer is the peak season for picking and cropping tobacco, and the days were long. Working with the sun beating down on my neck and sweat pouring down my face from bending over pulling tobacco leaves was exhausting. Just wiping my forehead was no easy task because my hands were covered with a quarter inch of tobacco wax. The smell and the sticky feeling stayed with me for days. But harder than the heat or handling the tobacco was the endlessness of the labor. To a young kid, the rows of green tobacco seemed infinite. I was constantly looking up to see how much farther I had to go to get to the end of a row. The rows could stretch a quarter-mile long, and there were often hundreds and hundreds of rows.

That's what I did during my summers. I won't romanticize it. It wasn't a lot of fun.

My grandparents had done this summer after summer for over fifty years. Even during a good season, they wouldn't make much money. It wasn't until the fall when the crops were harvested that they'd clear a couple thousand dollars. Most of that was used to pay the previous year's debt.

I'm not trying to tell a "rags to riches," "small-town kid does good" kind of story. I'm not seeking sympathy or admiration for where I came from. There are countless people who have overcome tougher circumstances than I did.

But like many who grew up with little, I acquired a foundation and some important principles that served me well later on. I learned it's alright to work hard. I learned the importance of having the strength to go the distance. I learned that you treat people with dignity and respect, even if you knew they wouldn't treat you the same in return.

I also understood that my family wanted something better for me and my siblings. They not only wanted it, they believed it was possible. My grandparents and parents never despaired; they always seemed optimistic. Picking tobacco didn't define them, and it wouldn't define me. And their quiet confidence in the possibility that life would get better was the most important lesson I took away from my own long, hot summers.

Although I never could bring myself to take up smoking. *(OK, maybe a cigar every once in a while).*

I also remember the first time the idea of joining the Army occurred to me. I was about 12 years old, sitting in my grandparents' family room. My uncle had come to visit us. He was a soldier who had just returned from a year in Vietnam. I remember how excited we were to have him back. We'd gathered in the family room around a wood-burning heater *(yes, we really did burn wood for heat)* and we were asking him question after question. Mostly, we wanted to know what he was going to do now that he was home from the war. Even at 12, I could tell his response left the grown-ups stunned. "I volunteered to go back to Vietnam," he said.

I was stunned too, although the basis of my reaction was different from that of the older folks in the room. I'd just lost my fishing buddy.

I remember my grandfather asking, "Why in the world would you want to go back to Vietnam when you've already done your time there?"

My uncle, who was a very serious man, said, "Well, I'm a soldier and the other soldiers I served with are my friends. They're still there, so I need to be there with them and to serve my country."

My uncle then looked over at me and told me the Army was a good place to make a difference with your life. His willingness to go back to Vietnam and passion for serving others had a profound influence on me. The very real controversies and debates about the war weren't a part of my 12-year old life after all.

My uncle's words have stayed with me to this day. I owe him a tremendous thank you. He was right about the Army at least, and about a lot of other things too. He is now enjoying retirement in Pleasant Shade, Virginia.

Right after high school, I left Virginia and moved north to Newark, New Jersey, where I got a job washing dishes in a cafeteria. One day, the manager asked me to get on my knees and scrub the baseboards along the floors. I did what he asked, because, after all, it was a job and I was getting paid.

Somehow, though, scrubbing those baseboards got to me in a way that picking tobacco hadn't. After work, I was sitting at the nearby bus stop, on my way home, with tears in my eyes. "Do I want to scrub floors and wash dishes the rest of my life?" I was thinking of my family and their hopes for me.

The bus stop was across from the Army recruiting station. I walked in, remembering what my uncle had shared with me years earlier. I was greeted by a Sergeant First Class Freeman. He was a tall, slender young man in his early thirties who looked to me like a model soldier and citizen. Several weeks later, he enlisted me in the U.S. Army. I was 17 years old.

When I received my first paycheck (about $321) during basic training at Fort Knox, Kentucky, I thought, "Man, is this all I have to do to make this type of money?" I was young and I only planned to be in the Army for a short time.

42 years later, I was still there.

Once I completed basic training, I attended my Advance Individual Training (AIT) where I learned to be a cavalry scout, or a 19 Delta in 'Army-speak.' When I graduated, I received a check for $2,500 as an enlistment bonus. I kept $600 and gave $1900 to my grandparents to put plumbing and running water in their home.

Fast forward 42 years. Shortly after I retired from the Army, I was at a Baylor University football game. I was asked by a third grader sitting next to me. "Sir, have you held every rank in the Army?" A pretty simple question, and the answer was, "No, I hadn't." But it did make me think about how fortunate I was to have risen through the ranks from private to buck sergeant to lieutenant general.

It also reminded me how much the Army had done for me and my family.

As a private, a cavalry scout, I had the opportunity to dig fighting positions while carrying an M60 machine gun for miles. *(I loved it. Much easier than picking tobacco.)*

As a sergeant, I patrolled the border between East and West Germany during the Cold War.

As a captain, I commanded a company on the Trans-Korean Petroleum Pipeline, which was one of the most fascinating jobs I've ever had. I was 31 years old and our unit supported all U.S. forces in the northern part of the Republic of Korea with fuel.

As a colonel, I served in Afghanistan as the senior logistician in the country. The Army allowed me to lead the Joint Logistics Command in 2006–2007, which supported over 70 outposts and logistics and transportation nodes that enabled materiel shipment from ports in Pakistan and Northern Europe to over 35,000 U.S. and allied troops.

In 2008, as a young brigadier general, I was placed in charge of the Joint Munitions Command, in Rock Island, Illinois, which provided the majority of the U.S. military's ammunition. Our team oversaw 16 ammunition production and storage facilities across the U.S., while supporting the wars in Iraq and Afghanistan.

In my final Army job, I was the deputy commanding general of the U.S. Army Materiel Command (AMC), which is a $58 billion logistics enterprise, employing a workforce of over 120,000 soldiers, government civilians, and contractors. Although not widely known, AMC is a global organization, with a presence or economic impact in all 50 U.S. states and 152 countries. We were in charge of 23 arsenals, maintenance depots, and manufacturing plants; supported by a supply chain of over 11,000 vendors; with more than ten billion service parts in inventory, and an $11 billion annual operating budget.

All of the opportunities I had were due to the hard work and commitment of the Soldiers and Army Civilians I served with. They weren't 'mine' in any real way. It was the Army itself, as an institution, that allowed me to do so much over the years.

Back in July 1999, I took command of the 4th Forward Support Battalion, which is part of the Army's 4th Infantry Division, at Fort Hood, Texas.

Command of a battalion is significant in an Army career. I'd served under many commanders and as I was about to accept this responsibility, I wanted to distill what it meant to be in the U.S. Army, and specifically what it meant to be a logistician in the Army.

I carved out some time alone to think of words that would convey the unique ethos of an Army soldier and *logistician*. I came up with these:

We are warfighter logisticians and supporters. We are prepared to give the shirts off our backs and boots off our feet to support the fight; we will never say no as long as we have one gallon of gas or one bullet to give.

The operative word in that motto is *give*.

No matter what kind of organization they serve, whether in the military, government, or the business world, logisticians are full-time, professional "givers." They provide the things—equipment, parts, technology, maintenance, transportation, food, water, shelter, electricity, ammunition, medical supplies—that allow others to do their jobs. Great logisticians always focus on helping and providing for someone else. More than anything, that's the single quality that leads to success in this unique field. And if you are a leader of logisticians, you have to ensure that same quality permeates your entire organization.

Today, logistics is widely recognized as a vital, complex, and rapidly changing field–in the military and in business (One might even say it's a "hot" specialty right now).

I wrote this book because I believe the lessons the Army taught me as a logistician and supply-chain professional may be of value to others in this field. Soldiers deployed around the world, first-line supervisors of commercial production facilities, mid-level business managers, and seasoned CEOs all need to understand global supply chains and how logistics drive their organizations.

There are literally thousands of books about the military and about leadership. There are even hundreds about logistics. I wanted to write a book that combined lessons about logistics, leadership, and business for all those who aspire to positions of responsibility in this growing field.

My hope is that as you read it, these lessons will do as much for you as they did for me in my own career.

CHAPTER 1:

WHY DO THIS?
(When 'Service' becomes a 'Calling')

Maybe it's my childhood and my grandmother always telling me to treat people kindly. Maybe it was having the right mentors throughout my career. It may be for any number of reasons, but what I've learned over the years is that the most important instinct for a leader is to serve the people they lead and the organization they belong to.

The famous management theorist Peter Drucker often advised business leaders to manage members of their workforce as if they were "volunteers" rather than paid employees. Drucker knew that most people are not solely motivated by money.

In the military, every single service member is a volunteer. The draft ended in January 1973, and since then, the military has had to recruit and motivate people to serve in uniform. Of course, civilian organizations are no different. Nobody drafts anyone to work at Apple, Google, Amazon, Wal-Mart, or a small business. And nobody drafts people to be teachers, police officers, nurses or firefighters. At some point, your employees have to want to be a part of your organization— even if it was only on the first day they showed up for work!

Serving the people who work for you is one of the most important and overlooked roles of leaders, at any level, and in any organization. I would often say to my soldiers and civilian employees that, "I work for you."

It took me a while in the Army to recognize the importance of serving the people under you. In fact, for many years, my primary motivation to stay in the Army and to prove that I could be a leader had come from experiencing a pretty bad example of leadership.

As a young buck sergeant, a cavalry scout, early in my career, we were out on maneuvers in Fort Hood, Texas. It was a cold night and there was a break in the training. Some of my fellow platoon members and I were standing around a fire trying to stay warm *(mostly without success)*. We were joking around a bit when my platoon leader walked by.

Now, in the Army, a platoon leader is usually a junior officer around the rank of lieutenant. To a young enlisted soldier, though, there really is no such thing as a "junior" officer. They were all senior to me, and this one was the first officer in my chain of command. He was responsible for leading our platoon, maintaining morale and discipline, and making sure that we would be ready for combat. In short, he was a leader I looked up to, and one of the first officers I'd encountered in my brief Army career.

As he walked by, I was telling my friends that someday I wanted to be a sergeant major (the highest enlisted rank a soldier can aspire to and a position of tremendous respect in the Army). The lieutenant, overhearing what I'd said, turned to me and declared in front of my platoon mates, "Wyche, you will NEVER be NOTH-ING." Believe me, he was not joking.

Those words, while definitely not the worst I'd heard over the years, lit a long, slow fire under me, although I did not fully realize it until much later. Many times after that night, when I faced a tough task, I'd be thinking about that lieutenant and needed to prove to myself how mistaken he was. That said, "negative motivation," which in this case was proving someone else wrong and holding on to that for years, is not a great reason for staying in the Army. As I was gradually given more and more leaderships jobs by the Army, I really did need to stop and figure out whether I truly wanted to do the kinds of things the Army had in store for me. The good news is that I never experienced another incident quite like the one with that platoon leader.

It became clear to me that my real purpose—my "positive motivator"—was that I wanted to serve alongside soldiers. I loved soldiers and the kinds of people who were in the Army. I enjoyed building and being a part of teams.

17

So, my purpose – my 'calling' – became to serve the soldiers and people I worked with.

Now, the notion of serving your employees may seem counter-intuitive at first, since many new managers and supervisors concentrate on how employees serve them and the organization. However, all good leaders (and especially logisticians) know they are responsible for ensuring that their team members have what they need to accomplish their tasks, whether that's equipment, funding, training, or support from other parts of the organization. Good leaders come to work every day thinking: *"How can I serve those who work for me? And what do they need to be more effective, improve their performance, and increase their job satisfaction?"*

And you can't answer questions like that unless you are continually "talking and walking." By that, I mean talking to your team members and walking around their work spaces. There is simply no leadership substitute for engagement and visibility.

When I walked through my organization to visit soldiers and civilians, many would share with me that their leaders had never visited them at their workstations. Not once.

I found that absolutely amazing.

By talking and walking, I learned about their families and the important parts of their lives, outside of work. I learned their favorite foods, hobbies, and sports teams. *(Talking about the Minnesota Vikings has always been therapeutic for me).*

In one case, a proud father told me his son had been accepted into West Point, the U.S. Military Academy. That short conversation started a long relationship with the father and his son. In fact, when the young man graduates from West Point, I plan to be at the ceremony. Those kind of relationships are invaluable.

I also learned from talking and walking, whether in Afghanistan or at an Army headquarters, the true impact visible, engaged leaders have on the success of an organization.

I did these 'talks and walks' at least weekly.

And I always tried to *listen* more than *talk.*

When I asked questions, they ranged from a friendly *"How are you getting along?"* to a more goal-oriented *"Do you understand our organization's priorities?"* Although I never wanted to seem like I was quizzing people.

During these walk-throughs, I almost always found something important to share with other senior leaders and staff members; a problem we needed to address; or a success we needed to reinforce.

I learned that the newest, best 'app' or 'communication tool' is still face-to-face conversation *(Whenever that's possible, anyway).* As tempting as it might be, you can't always lead through the phone, email, a website, or social media.

And despite the many leadership books that highlight the importance of 'leadership by walking around,' I'm still surprised more leaders don't regularly walk out and talk to their employees. As we say in the Army, it should be 'SOP' ('Standard Operating Procedure').

Lieutenant General William G. Pagonis, who led the massive U.S. supply effort during the Gulf War in 1990–1991, was a big believer in getting out with the troops. He could get a better feel for what was going on.

"People contribute most willingly when they are shown that their contribution has value," he observed. "Having the leader show up makes that point forcefully." He understood the value of "the personal touch."[1]

Soldiers and civilian employees often just want someone to listen to them. I got some of the most useful logistics and supply-chain information while chatting in line at the Post Exchange, at the mess hall, or at the gym.

When I commanded the U.S. Army Combined Arms Support Command (CASCOM) in Fort Lee, Virginia, one of our Command's responsibilities was educating military and civilian logisticians of all ranks. I made it a point to speak with them in the classroom, during physical fitness training, in the dining facility, and wherever else I could. In fact, I probably became something of a pest. I also encouraged all our leaders to be similarly visible.

1 Lt. General William G. Pagonis, Moving Mountains: Lessons in Leadership and Logistics from the Gulf War (Boston: Harvard Business School Press, 1992), pp. 166–167.

I remember how visibility paid real dividends for us. Often when things were not going well.

For example, during the 16-day government shutdown in October 2013, many of our Army civilian employees had to make difficult financial decisions. Should they buy groceries or pay their rent?

We worked hard to make all of our leaders even more visible – before, during and after – in what was a trying time for our civilian team members. They appreciated our compassion and when the furlough was over, CASCOM recovered with minimal disruption, in part, because many of our civilians had personally seen us, face to face.

I'd also witnessed the value of this approach in Afghanistan.

As a senior logistician there from 2006 to 2007, the command I led was responsible for a huge supply-chain operation supporting over 35,000 troops.

I remember visiting a remote outpost in the northern mountains of the country. The terrain was both beautiful and brutal at the same time.

I flew in by helicopter and met with the leader, Lieutenant Colonel Fenty. After he gave me a quick overview of his operations, he took me around to meet his troops.

I was amazed at the resilience of these soldiers. They'd been deployed in the most austere conditions imaginable. However, as I walked through the outpost, I noticed several of their uniforms were worn out from conducting combat patrols in the harsh terrain and climate. Frankly, they were just plain raggedy. You could see their underwear through rips in their pants.

Out of the corner of my eye, I noticed a couple of soldiers burning something. I assumed it was trash. But when I walked over to talk to them and asked them what they were doing, they replied that they were *burning their own human waste*. One looked at me and smiled: "Sir, it's not a lot of fun burning shit, but it has to be done."

As I wrapped up my visit, another soldier approached me. "Sir, I have something to ask you," he said. I expected him to ask for working toilets. But instead the young man looked at me and said, "Sir, do you think you could get us some pecan pies for the holidays?"

"Sure," I replied. I hadn't been expecting that.

All that he was enduring and the only thing he wanted was pecan pies. There was no way we were going to disappoint him.

Shortly thereafter within a few days that mountain outpost received new uniforms and twenty pecan pies.

Tragically, several weeks after my visit, Lieutenant Colonel Fenty and nine others were killed in a helicopter accident. The outpost was later re-named Forward Operating Base Fenty.

The point is that you need to get out among your troops and find out what's going on. The higher up you climb, the harder this simple task will get. In Afghanistan, my team and I had to know what was in the supply and distribution pipelines—from the big industrial facilities outside the country to the remotest outposts in

Afghanistan—at all times. And with many of our biggest challenges occurring after the supplies and equipment had arrived in Afghanistan, having engaged, visible leadership there was invaluable.

Takeaways:

- Value your soldiers, employees, and their families
- Engaged and <u>visible</u> leadership matters
- Know what's important to the customer *(Even if it's Pecan Pies)*

CHAPTER 2:

HOW TO GET GOOD AT IT
(The Big Picture and the Little Details)

Point blank, being a logistician (or a leader of logisticians) can often seem like a thankless job.

Whether you're coordinating the logistics or supply chains for the government, the military, or in business, it takes a certain mix of personality characteristics like a thick skin, the ability to keep your eye on both the big picture and the little details, and a commitment to serving an organization selflessly. If you have a strong need to be the center of attention, the job of a logistician is probably not for you.

To use a football analogy, the logistician is like the center on the offensive line. You are going to have your hands on the ball for just about every play, and the game can't go on without you, but you won't get the attention that the quarterback, running backs, or wide receivers receive. In fact, when you do get attention, it usually means you've been given a penalty.

I use the phrases *big picture* and *little details* for a reason. Over the course of your career, whatever line of work you're in, you might hear people describe themselves as "big picture types" or conversely say "I'm more of a details kind of guy." These are sometimes viewed as mutually exclusive traits. You're either one or the other, or at least much more comfortable with one than the other.

Logisticians, however, don't get to choose sides.

This might come as a surprise to some people, even to those who've been in this profession for many years. Logisticians have traditionally been thought of as members of the "detail team," which is understandable. After all, logisticians are usually absorbed with the complicated task of getting exactly what an organization needs to a specific place at precisely the right time in accordance with an elaborate plan. Logisticians can't be "*close enough*" types. We need to know the answer to questions like: "How many gallons of JP-8 fuel are needed for a battalion-size task force to conduct a 500-mile tactical road march from eastern to southern Afghanistan? And when and where will the convoy require refueling operations?"

It's the logistician's job to know those kinds of details. The truth is, most logisticians love details and love being the experts who are ready with the right answer.

However, logisticians are also responsible for understanding how all those details fit together to achieve a broader objective. It's vital for a logistician to look away from all those details, scan the horizon, and see events from a strategic perspective. Military logisticians have to deliver from "factory to foxhole." Understanding logistics from the strategic to tactical levels is easier said than done. It's a unique skill acquired over time through experience, reading, and reflecting on how logistics enables military commanders to operate on the modern battlefield, or how logistics enables a business to function most efficiently and effectively. The logistician who can move quickly from the strategic to the tactical, and from the global to the local, without missing a beat is invaluable – and represents the future of this profession.

So, in addition to a thick skin, what are the qualities that make for a great logistician?

Some character traits are fundamental to success in any profession. These include courage, character, integrity, honesty, a willingness to work hard, competence, and self-discipline.

However, there are certain other traits that mark the very best logisticians. In no particular order, they include:

They anticipate: Good logisticians are natural "futurists." They need to understand, visualize, and predict what lies ahead, and then prepare for a wide range of possibilities. In the military, the logistician has to anticipate what the commander will need, and when and where they'll need it, before the commander does. Logisticians need to keep one eye on the present and the other on what's next. No general *(or CEO of a business)* wants their options limited by a lack of logistics. Because no organization can afford to have everything, everywhere, all the time, effective anticipation ensures that the most critical material will be there when it's needed most. Anticipation prevents the logistician from being jerked around by events outside their control.

I once served with Colonel Chris Toner (now retired) when he led Task Force Catamount during Operation Mountain Thrust in Afghanistan. During this operation, Toner later wrote, "Sustainment commanders and staffs at all levels visualized future operations, identified required support and implemented sustainment that supported the tactical commanders' operations. Despite the distances, terrain, and overall austerity of the environment I felt like I always had the ability to maintain, protect, and sustain forces." This is what we mean by anticipation for logisticians – and the kind of assessment we want to receive from battlefield commanders.

They're responsive: The best logisticians not only anticipate the future, they're responsive rather than reactive. It's impossible to overstate the importance of responsiveness and speed in today's military environment, and the same is true in the business world. The U.S. armed forces have demonstrated they can deploy rapidly around the world and then sustain their operations. Moving fast gives you an advantage over your opponent or competitors. The organization that responds to changing circumstances quickly is able to leverage its strengths, exploit its competitor's vulnerabilities, and seize opportunities at a consistently faster pace than others.

They integrate: Logistical knowledge and skill are all for naught if they're not integrated into your organization's overall plan. Fitting the pieces of the logistics and supply chain puzzle together, and then integrating them into the organization's larger mission so that it achieves its goals, is a skill highly valued by generals and CEOs. Oftentimes, logistics and supply chains are almost afterthoughts and not given the attention they deserve. The aggressive and forward-thinking logistician ensures that all aspects of logistics are fully integrated into the organization's larger plan.

To achieve this integration, a skilled logistician should have a seat at the organization's leadership table. As a battalion commander during a maneuver exercise at Fort Hood, Texas, I walked into the brigade operations center to give the daily commander's update. Normally about 40 individuals attended. There were six other commanders present, and all of them had designated seats. But I did not. I looked at the brigade operations officer, who was a major, and in a very firm, stern voice, I said, "Am I not part of this brigade combat team?" The brigade commander, Colonel Anderson, then said to the operations officer, "Where is Lieutenant Colonel Wyche's seat?" That may sound a little arrogant – but it's often necessary for logisticians to ensure they're 'on the leadership team.' The Commander ensuring his logistician had a seat at the table was one small signal that we would be fully integrated into the Brigade's planning efforts.

They're flexible: Good logisticians are willing to change course and alter plans in light of new facts or data. As an Army logistician, I never saw a plan or operation that didn't require adjustments. Most of them required lots of them. It's a safe assumption that your plan will change, and logisticians must be flexible to meet the changing needs of the people they support. If you're not, you won't be in the support business for long. Trust me.

They're resilient: As a logistician, you will face plenty of unexpected situations. Your ability to handle unforeseen setbacks or criticism without allowing either to overwhelm you is a must.

Maintaining a proper perspective when things go wrong—while remaining positive, confident, and resolute in pursuit of your goal—will gain you respect from your subordinates, peers, and superiors.

They're tactful: We all know the golden rule: "treat people like you want to be treated." Everyone deserves dignity and respect. Soldiers care about how much you know, but they care more about how you treat them. Same for most people. Treating others—whether they're your seniors, juniors, or peers—with a respect that recognizes the inherent worth of all people will always serve you well. I've also found that approaching conflict and difficult, emotional, or hostile situations with firmness while remaining calm and in control of my temper enhances my chances of success.

Few want to work for a boss or around coworkers who are frantic or frazzled all the time. You need to have a level head and act calmly during crises *(which, granted, may require some acting ability).* Calmness lends itself to sound decision-making and clear thinking and instills confidence in your abilities among those around you. In Afghanistan, I witnessed several of my battalion commanders lose their cool in front of their staffs or troops. While combat is one of the most stressful environments you can experience, few things are more important in combat than the commander having a calm, confident demeanor. After observing more than one episode of this kind of behavior, I called all of my battalion commanders to my operations center and told them that only when they saw me lose my own temper did they have permission to lose theirs.

This is hardly an exhaustive list. However, the above traits are essential to being a good logistician. Just as importantly, they're essential to being a good leader and just a plain-old good human being.

Some of these traits can take years to hone and develop. That said, I believe you can take active steps in the next 90-days to become a better logistics leader. 90 days may not seem like a lot of time, but it's enough to turn your career, attitude, and aptitude around as a logistician.

Here are four quick ways to become a better one in the next 90 days:

✓ Commit to fully understanding and reading (or re-reading) the mission and vision statements of your command, business, or government program. If you're in the military, you need to understand the campaign and strategic plans (most military units have both) that direct your command's actions. You need to also be fully familiar with your commander's guidance and intent. Do the same for the military units or work groups or offices at the next two higher echelons in your chain of command or company hierarchy. Devote time to closing the door and ensuring that you have a firm grasp of these and your group's role in supporting them. Find time to discuss and debate them with your peers to ensure that you have a shared view of these important materials.

✓ Make sure you know more than your commander or boss about the logistical needs of your unit, company, or agency. While your boss will likely always have a broader perspective and greater understanding of the overall mission of your command or organization, you should make a commitment to being the go-to logistics expert on your staff. Anticipate the logistics questions and concerns your boss will have for upcoming operations and ensure that you have coordinated, accurate, and up-to-date answers. This may seem obvious; however, it's surprising how many logisticians can't meet anticipatable requests for information, or how often the commander or boss has to inform them about logistics issues they should be on top of. Don't let that happen to you.

✓ Understand the current logistics limitations of your military unit, business, or agency. Ask yourself questions like, "what are the most critical supply and maintenance shortfalls at the moment?" and "If we had to respond to a contingency in the next 90 days, what would be our most important priority, and where would we likely need assistance?"

✓ For the next 90 days, don't let yourself complain about anything. It's all too easy to allow a culture of chronic griping, whining, grousing, and grumbling to permeate an organization. There is never a shortage of complaints in most military units, companies, and government departments. Don't be a part of it. This doesn't mean you should view the world through rose-colored glasses, or refrain from correcting things when they're wrong. As a leader and logistician, it just means you should have a consistently positive and confident attitude. Try it. Go 90 days without uttering a single complaint and see if it doesn't change your perspective and the views others have of you.

After 90 days, I'm willing to wager that you will be a better logistician (and leader)!

Takeaways:

*   You're not the center of attention
*   Understand both the little details and the big picture
*   Develop the traits critical to your role
*   You can be a better logistician (and leader) in just 90 days

CHAPTER 3:

I WISH I'D PLANNED FOR THAT

(The Military Decision-Making Process)

All organizations require sound planning and decision-making. I was first introduced to the Army's rigorous approach to planning and decision-making during a six-month, advanced course for logistics officers. Most of us were captains and looking forward to assuming command of a company (for the *'non-military reader,'* that's usually a unit of somewhere between 60 and 150 soldiers – depending on the mission). A successful tour as a company commander is one of the most important leadership milestones for an Army officer. Do well and you might be given more responsibility down the road. Do poorly, and you will likely be encouraged to work on your civilian résumé.

Up until then, I hadn't given the subject of planning a lot of thought. Although all junior officers are taught some elements of planning early on, as a young lieutenant and NCO, my focus was on leading small units and just "making things happen." That was hard enough. Fortunately, as a mental tool, the Army formalizes the process of leading small units into eight standard "troop-leading" steps. They are committed to memory by most NCOs and young officers:

Receive the Mission

Issue the Warning Order

Make a Tentative Plan

Initiate Movement

Conduct Reconnaissance

Complete the Plan

Issue the Order

Supervise

Although these troop-leading steps include *planning*, plans at this level are fairly simple and straightforward. For the most part, more complex plans in the Army involving bigger units and the execution of larger operations were above my pay grade at the time. More experienced Army leaders were the ones who came up with these "big" plans. These officers and NCOs were assigned to higher headquarters than mine, so I had minimal interaction with them. As a result, I lacked a well-informed understanding of the complexity of what these 'planners' did for a living.

However, at the six-month logistics advanced course, held at Fort Lee, Virginia, planning was a major portion of the curriculum. In fact, planning is one of those topics the military just can't get enough of. Along with the other officers in my class, I was motivated, ambitious, and eager to learn. In fact, my ambition might have come on a little too strongly.

At that time in the Army, the early 1980s, it was widely accepted that to prove yourself as a captain, you not only needed a successful tour as a company commander, but also a master's degree. I was fairly confident I would do well as a company commander, because I felt the Army had provided me with the right experiences, training, and professional education. However, while attendance at the logistics advanced course was worth a few graduate credits, it definitely wouldn't get me a degree.

About two weeks into the course, we had just finished a lecture on logistics planning at the "theater" level *(theater in Army-speak usually means a large area of operations)*, and the instructor gave us a 10-minute break. I walked down to talk with him, fired up with a smile on my face. I asked him for his recommendations on the best way for a young officer to earn a master's degree.

Well, I didn't get the answer I was looking for. What I got was more of a butt-chewing. The instructor looked at me and barked, *"Lieutenant Wyche, you do not need to worry about how to get a master's degree. You need to focus on learning and mastering the military decision-making process!"*

Having knocked me and my academic pretensions back a bit, he then handed me a sheet of paper that succinctly displayed the entire military decision-making process and told me to put it on my refrigerator and in any other place in my house where I could see it. He added that at any time I thought I needed a master's degree to succeed as an Army captain, I should instead read and commit to memory the contents of that sheet of paper.

It looked a lot like this:

Receipt of Mission (or a "Warning Order")
Mission Analysis
Course of Action Development
Course of Action Analysis
Course of Action Comparison
Course of Action Approval
Orders Production
Rehearsal
Execution and Assessment

Although discouraged by his remarks—and a little bit ticked off that I needed to hear them—being a good soldier, I took the sheet of paper and walked away.

And then, I did exactly what he told me to do. Eighteen years later, I realized that his was some of the best advice I've ever received.

I worked hard at learning what was on that paper and it has served me well ever since. More detailed and comprehensive than the "troop-leading steps" I'd already learned, the military decision-making process, or MDMP, was my introduction to a model for planning, getting things done, and solving problems in a complex organization like the Army—an organization which has a seemingly infinite number of moving parts that interact with one another. In some ways, these interactions are very carefully orchestrated. However, in other ways they are as unpredictable as the weather. The purpose of the MDMP, in part, is to manage this "fog of war" while keeping the organization on track. Just as importantly, the MDMP is not only a model that results in an actionable, formal plan, it is a model for finding solutions to the everyday problems that arise in most organizations.

The military decision-making process provides a structure for commanders and organizations as a whole to work collectively through a coordinated series of steps to accomplish a task. The process can be used in a deliberate fashion over a period of months or in a crisis where you are working to build a plan in only hours or days.

I know what you might be thinking—that any structured process with a predefined series of steps is probably too rigid and inflexible to be useful in the messy real world. In part, you are right—but *only* in part.

You have all heard the famous quote (by now a cliché) *"No plan survives first contact with the enemy."*[2] It's attributed to the great nineteenth-century Chief of the German General Staff Helmuth von Moltke (usually appended with the title "the Elder" because his nephew and namesake was later also chief of the German general staff in the period prior to World War I). A contemporary and disciple of Carl von Clausewitz, von Moltke knew a thing or two about planning, enemy contact, and the fog of war. He saw combat

---

2 "No plan of operations reaches with any certainty beyond the first encounter with the enemy's main force." Kriegsgechichtliche Einzelschriften (1880); often quoted as, 'No plan survives first contact with the enemy,' Oxford Essential Quotations, 4th Ed.

and assisted in planning the German army's strategy in its wars with the Austrians, Danish, and French throughout the period of 1822 to 1897.

So, if no plan survives contact with the enemy, why do we have them?

Well, another quote, this one often attributed in various forms to General Dwight D. Eisenhower, sheds some additional light on the subject: *"In preparing for battle, I have always found that plans are useless, but planning is indispensable."*[3]

Therein lies the vital distinction.

After having almost daily interaction with the military decision-making process for many years now, it has confirmed for me that approaching problems in a structured, deliberate manner, one that involves each key element of an organization, makes you less likely to make planning mistakes, less likely to forget critical actions in the heat of a crisis, and far more likely to get a result close to what you intended.

Using the MDMP, staff members acquire, monitor, synchronize, and refine information across their areas of responsibility—whether that's personnel, communications, finance, logistics, or anything else. The planning process guides all involved as they gather information, identify options, and turn those options into recommendations and potential courses of action. The MDMP, as complex as it can seem to those who are just learning it, is where bright ideas

3   1957 November 19, The Wall Street Journal, Meeting the Unknown, Quote Page 14, Column 1, New York. (ProQuest) & 1962, Six Crises by Richard M. Nixon, Chapter: Khrushchev, Quote Page 253, A Cardinal Edition: Pocket Books, New York.

either grow into actions on the battlefield or are replaced with better ideas.

In short, it works. It works whether you're solving a simple problem, such as delivering supplies to a small unit, or developing a truck strategy for the entire U.S. Army (a planning problem I was personally involved with).

However, even in the military where the MDMP is used over and over again, we don't always employ it as effectively as we should. As a result, we often find ourselves wondering why we don't get the results we're looking for.

Understanding the MDMP is extremely important for a military professional. It's a framework for thinking through problems regardless of their complexity. It provides a vocabulary and shared mindset for a military command as it drafts plans to achieve objectives. The MDMP allows the disparate parts of a global organization like the U.S. military to build a common culture of problem-solving applicable wherever service members may find themselves. Moreover, even though most civilian organizations do not refer to their planning processes as the MDMP, the elements of effective planning are often similar.

The Nuances of Implementation

Prior to the Gulf War in 1990–1991, many logisticians at the battalion level and higher would have benefited from more extensive education and experience in MDMP, as this sort of systematic decision-making process is needed to execute operations on the scale of Desert Shield and Desert Storm. Speaking for myself, serving at the battalion level in the late 1990s and early 2000s, even though I'd been trained in the MDMP at the advanced course for logistics officers at Fort Lee and at the Combined Arms and Services Staff School at Fort Leavenworth, Kansas, I had still been learning a lot on the fly. I knew how to do planning at the battalion level, but I hadn't acquired the skill set to successfully plan larger operations.

While I was familiar with some of the logistics parts of creating a good plan, it was often assumed in the Army that those who worked in the 'G3' staff section (operations) or the 'G5' staff section (plans) would have overall responsibility for overseeing the execution of the MDMP. Too many people 'assumed' the full-time planners and operators would do the lion's share of integrating the logistics requirements in the plan. While a logistician often worked directly in the G3 and G5 staffs, we were not always able to shape the decision-making process in a way that fully used our logistics expertise to support the commander's intent and mission.

Understanding the nuances of the MDMP and how the drafting of a plan evolves over time is both an art and a science. The chain of command, along with the relationships between the different military staff sections, can be learned from reading military orders and doctrine. However, the more valuable knowledge comes from understanding the interests and perspectives of the different staff sections – and the numerous briefings, working groups, cells, and planning teams that quickly emerge to analyze issues or to examine the details of particular problems. Understanding when and how to engage throughout the MDMP is the mark of the skilled planning professional.

Indeed, knowing when to raise an issue during a meeting (or when to raise it after the meeting in a one-on-one session); knowing how to present an idea; knowing in what sequence key staff members should be engaged; anticipating questions and developing clear answers; and building a consensus are critical (if unwritten) parts of the planning process. The most successful staff officers have mastered the knowledge of when to *speak up*, when to *step up*, and when to *shut up*.

The ability to discern and closely observe the personalities of the staff and commanders involved in building a plan shouldn't be dismissed as a "soft" skill. Nor should recognizing the different perspectives and approaches they take to the MDMP. Many people can come up with bright ideas and great suggestions. But doing the hard, painstaking, and sometimes frustrating work of getting bright ideas and suggestions through a large military staff and into a final plan is what defines a truly valuable staff officer. This skill is not easy to acquire and the military has worked hard to incorporate the MDMP into many of its professional military education (PME) courses. In fact, most military students attending PME courses will participate in exercises that simulate the complex decision-making, planning, and coordination that occur throughout the MDMP.

These exercises also simulate the sorts of relationships, give-and-take, and disagreements that may occur.

It is tempting when pressed for time, or when a particular course of action seems obvious, to skip or shortchange parts of the MDMP. This is usually a recipe for error, or worse. It often results in a commander or staff having to "wing it" when problems that could have been foreseen were not adequately prepared for. Believe me, *after* you find yourself inside a minefield is not the time to realize you needed a plan to avoid it.

Although structured in its approach to planning and problem-solving, the MDMP has the flexibility to adapt to virtually any circumstance. The different steps in the process can be executed simultaneously and it can be shaped to optimum advantage by savvy leaders experienced in its application. Leadership is key throughout the MDMP—it facilitates constructive debate, open discussion, timely decision-making, and development of actionable recommendations.

Recognizing shortcomings in the ability of senior officers to plan and make decisions in complex, constantly changing environments, the Army established the School of Advanced Military Studies (SAMS) in the early 1980s. Still emerging from the bitter experience of Vietnam, several of the Army's most senior officers sought to create a cadre of highly trained planners and analytical thinkers who had not only demonstrated expertise in their respective areas of warfare, but who also showed the potential to understand how U.S. and allied military forces could be better integrated to achieve national security objectives. The Army wanted to "seed" itself with a group of adaptive majors, lieutenant colonels, and colonels who could see beyond the specific skills they had acquired. It needed leaders who could assess how military force would be used in increasingly uncertain environments and how military officers could arrive at better decisions and improve their recommendations to civilian leaders.

SAMS quickly grew to recruit and attract some of the most talented officers in the Army, in the other services – and among our allies. Today, its curriculum is recognized as a global standard in the training of decision-making, analysis, risk management, and planning skills. This elite group of SAMS alumni are often referred to as "Jedi Knights" around the Department of Defense, a term that alludes to their unique skills and stature. Many SAMS graduates are routinely sought out by senior commanders to join their staffs as planning for a major military operation commenced. In fact, I've looked specifically for SAMS graduates to take advantage of their planning and analytical ability.

Some Personal Lessons in the MDMP

Nearly two decades of the war in Afghanistan, Iraq, and elsewhere have forced the Army to become better at using the MDMP.

However, the skills involved are perishable. In the Army, that means that colonels, lieutenant colonels, sergeant's major, and master sergeants must take the time to train those under their wing in the execution of the MDMP so that these skills are not lost. Continual training is the foundation of our combat edge, and making sure our soldiers benefit from the combat experience of those who have "been there and done that" is critical to our ability to learn faster than our enemies.

I truly gained an appreciation for the need for detailed planning while serving as the chief logistics programmer in the Pentagon in 2004. The MDMP provided me and my team a framework to think through the complex problem of meeting the needs of America's armed forces step-by-step, from identifying key problems to recommending solutions.

One of our top priorities was developing a new truck strategy for the Army. Also known as the tactical wheeled vehicle strategy, it needed to satisfy the Army's operational needs—in Afghanistan, Iraq, and in other countries—while modernizing our vehicles to become a more capable force. In an organization the size of the Army, which had over 42,000 vehicles that could be categorized as "trucks," this was an enormous undertaking and one that had an effect on just about every part of the service. I've always tried hard to be a positive guy, but after taking an initial look at the size and scope of this project, failure definitely *did* seem like a possibility. In fact, if we didn't come up with a strategy quickly, failure was imminent.

Fortunately, one of the best pieces of advice I received at the start of the effort was from Lieutenant General Benjamin Griffin, the Army's chief programmer, who said, *"Larry, just rely on the MDMP and you won't fail."* And he was right. It also helped that Joe Mata, a retired colonel, was assigned to our team; he was exceptionally bright and used the MDMP to its fullest.

After receiving our orders to develop the new truck strategy, we conducted a thorough mission analysis focusing on the vehicles' requirements, capability shortfalls, costs, and other variables. We did this analysis in coordination with key commands and programs in the Army. We then developed, analyzed, and compared possible courses of action, with the participation of Army leaders who had a vested interest in the project. Among the critical facts that drove our analysis was that the current pace of Army operations caused substantial wear and tear to our aging vehicles, and that this pace would likely continue. We balanced a variety of competing factors in developing possible courses of action, such as the need to support current operations and reduce operating costs while also modernizing our vehicle fleet. We used several criteria to assess the strength of each course of action to include: vehicle performance, force protection (i.e. could Soldiers survive and fight in these vehicles), mobility, cost, and schedule. The potential courses of action varied according to how many vehicles were restored, recapitalized, and upgraded, or replaced with new vehicles and a new system. We briefed senior Army leaders on the pluses and minuses of these options. To gain the approval of Army leaders on a course of action, we had to build a consensus—no easy task—which involved educating them on these pluses and minuses as well as on the risks of doing nothing. We also had to garner support from the Office of the Secretary of Defense and Congress. Our argument that the new tactical wheeled vehicle strategy offered the best value helped bring the participants to an agreement. Through frank discussion, we ultimately reached a consensus among all the parties and our new truck strategy was approved. Production of vehicles was then ordered.

My point is, the MDMP works whether you are planning the logistics for a Company of 120 soldiers headed out on movement to contact mission, or creating an Army-wide strategy for the maintenance and acquisition of more than 42,000 vehicles. Whether the problems are big and complicated or small and more manageable, the MDMP stays the same.

Takeaways:

* Systematic, deliberate planning is essential
* The MDMP should become 'second-nature'
* No matter the size of the problem, the process stays the same

CHAPTER 4:

TRAINING TO WIN
(There's a Model for that too)

It was Sunday afternoon a beautiful fall day in October 1983. After church, as with most Sundays during football season, my priority was watching the Minnesota Vikings. While enjoying the game with my wife, I received a phone call from the staff duty officer. I was a young second lieutenant serving as a platoon leader in the 267th Pipeline and Petroleum Company at Fort Lee, Virginia.

The company's staff duty officer informed me we had a fuel spill at one of the Fort's training sites. After briefly talking to my company commander, we activated the platoon's alert roster. About 15 soldiers reported to the company's headquarters within the hour. We received a quick situational update informing us that several thousand gallons of fuel had spilled. Immediately, we gathered the necessary equipment from our warehouse and then traveled to the training site. The spill was not as bad as first described; however, there was lots of work to be done.

As a young platoon leader, and this being my first assignment as an officer, I wanted to make a good impression for all the right reasons. Unfortunately, I did not.

The first order of business was to contain, pump, and upload the spilled fuel into our fuel tankers. After running the necessary hoses, and using 350 gallon fuel pumps, numerous attempts were made to start the pumps and not one of three pumps worked. It was my unit's responsibility to ensure these functioned and we'd failed. About 30 minutes into the clean-up, the brigade commander, battalion commander, and other installation leaders began to arrive at the site. We were very fortunate not to have the media there too.

How embarrassing.

Frankly, I let down my soldiers and the entire chain of command. As the platoon leader, my job was to ensure my soldiers and equipment were prepared. That Sunday, I learned several valuable and simple lessons starting with this one: always ensure your equipment is properly maintained and that my soldiers are trained and ready for the task at hand.

Also, I made the decision that day that I was going to work my butt off to be the best leader and logistician that I could be. I would never allow that lack of preparedness to happen again. We were lucky that day because our lives were not be in jeopardy. From that day on, and the many years that followed, I realized that my number one priority was preparing my soldiers, providing the best logistics support that I could, and bringing them back home to their loved ones.

I knew I was a much better leader than what I'd shown that day. Yet, I also understood that I had several shortcomings that I needed to confront honestly and quickly. Succeeding as a young "butter bar lieutenant" would require more hard work and lots of self-reflection to earn the trust of my platoon.

Luckily, only two weeks after the incident, my battalion commander, Lieutenant Colonel Steve Bliss, held a leader development class that focused on the Army's "Eight Step Training Model." The Army has many such models (like the MDMP we talked about in the last chapter) to guide leaders in a wide range of tasks and to be effective trainers of soldiers. Models like these are often the result of hard-earned lessons in combat and are a godsend for young NCOs and officers.

During the class, it was as if someone had turned a light switch on in my head. I saw that there was a training framework ready for me to use. It reminded me that the Army had been around for over two hundred years, and I almost never had to start any training task with a blank sheet of paper again.

So as not to make the same mistakes twice, I focused first on learning the training model and then teaching that model to my platoon. The model was simple and easily remembered, and its effectiveness has been proven over time in units all across the Army.

The eight steps in the training model are:

Step 1—Plan the training

A training plan has to start with an assessment of the unit's performance and proficiency. The best units deliver brutally honest assessments, allowing them to focus on training that targets weaknesses and reinforces strengths. One way the Army does this is through Quarterly Training Briefings, or QTBs. A QTB includes, among other things, a commander's presentation of their Mission Essential Task List (METL) assessment to a higher-level boss, accompanied by a candid (very candid) discussion. The meeting allows commanders to review past training and discuss future training plans. It also affords commanders the opportunity to highlight concerns, frictions, and resource shortfalls. Highlighting resource restrictions and shortfalls (some of which might be the responsibility of the higher command being briefed) is critical. For some, this can be a very painful briefing.

I actually enjoyed giving my boss the QTB because I knew my unit's training strengths and weaknesses. As a battalion commander, I kept my QTB and the list of tasks that I wanted to train my soldiers for on the right corner of my desk. As I observed training throughout the quarter, I would come back to my office and write down what I saw.

I remember one day when I went out to see how well our battalion was maintaining our vehicles, I noticed that, frankly, we weren't doing a good job. Some vehicle oil levels and tire air pressures were incorrect and we were not properly ordering repair parts for faulty equipment found during maintenance and inspections. So, my assessment was that we needed significant improvement. This was embarrassing for many of the leaders under me because one of the primary missions of maintenance and supply experts is to keep the entire brigade's vehicles up and running. Yet we weren't even doing a good job maintaining our *own* vehicles. Even though reporting this was painful to my battalion, I could look myself in the mirror knowing that I was honest.

Step 2—Train and certify leaders first

I'm not sure how commonly used phrases turn into clichés, but sometimes it's just because they're true. One of these clichés is "lead by example." It contains a lot of truth, and in fact it's the reason for step two in the training model. Whenever possible, *train and certify leaders first*. This accomplishes several important things. It generates confidence in leaders, and makes them better qualified to evaluate training. When soldiers see their leaders performing the same training they have to do, it builds a shared commitment in an organization. It's a way of saying *"We can – and will – do this together."*

Two of the most important examples of this in the Army are physical fitness and weapons training. As a young officer, it was very difficult for me to sleep at night knowing I had a physical fitness test or weapons qualification the next day. Junior soldiers closely watch how well their officers and NCOs do push-ups and sit-ups, how fast or slowly they run, and how accurately they can shoot. Do well, and you gained instant respect. Do poorly, and your soldiers would tolerate you—primarily because they had to.

Step 3—Conduct a training reconnaissance

In the military, leaders should take every opportunity to conduct a visual observation of a training site. Doing it will improve the execution and quality of training. During a site survey, leaders learn whether the site is suitable for the training, easily accessible in case of an emergency, and appropriate in a number of other ways. Often, military leaders don't have the luxury of visiting the training site. In those cases, using sand-table exercises and other forms to replicate the site can serve the same purpose.

Step 4—Issue an order for the training

In this step, leaders issue orders that establish clear tasks during the training, the conditions under which those tasks will take place, and the standards to be measured. This step includes a concept of operations that describes how training objectives will be met, and a concept of logistics for the training event. Although verbal orders can be issued, written orders are better here. They become a ready reference for all and can be quickly disseminated and reviewed, whereas verbal orders require leaders to constantly repeat information. Writing down the details of a training plan avoids this problem.

While serving as the 502d Support Battalion's operations officer, I received a well-deserved butt chewing from my battalion commander over my preparation of training orders. We were supporting a brigade during summer rotation at the National Training Center in the Mojave Desert in California. A critical task for an Army staff during any rotation is producing operations orders in a timely manner. As the battalion operations officer, my staff and I were responsible for this task. We received the brigade's order about twelve hours prior to executing a movement during the training. Within that twelve-hour window, lots of work had to be done to produce a battalion order that would not only guide the battalion's mission, but allow its companies time to receive the order and conduct their own planning. The Army has a rule called the "One-Third/Two-Thirds" rule. It means that a headquarters should spend one-third of the available time doing its own planning, while giving two-thirds of the time to subordinate units to do their planning and execution. Well, I violated that rule and spent too much time trying to produce a perfect battalion-level order, which meant that the companies had no time to plan and execute their own tasks. I learned that it's better to get a 70 percent plan into the hands of your team early than a 95 percent plan too late. This is true wherever you work.

Step 5—Rehearse the training

This step is crystal clear: rehearse, rehearse, and then rehearse some more. I can recall on the eve of deploying to Afghanistan in 2006, I had an office call with the division commander, Major General Lloyd Austin, who had already served in combat several times. During the meeting, I asked him if he had any advice prior to deploying. He replied, "You all are prepared and ready—just go execute like you have been trained." His guidance on training was equally succinct—rehearse again and again, in detail, whether for major combat operations or activities like receiving visiting dignitaries. I listened closely to his guidance, and it served us well in Afghanistan.

Step 6—Execute

Although a classroom can be an appropriate environment for training in the Army, it's not always preferred. Soldiers learn best by doing rather than by sitting in a classroom. We've got to get our hands dirty, for the most part, especially for tactical tasks. Training is about meeting and then getting better. Once a unit meets the standard, you have to increase the difficulty of the training under new conditions. For example, the same task might be done at night or in a different location; in a simulated nuclear, biological, or chemical environment; with a different leader in charge; or with any combination of such variables. These conditions reflect what units may face in actual combat or other operations.

Step 7—Evaluate Training and Conduct an After-Action Review (AAR)

It's important that you take the time to conduct AARs – or 'After-Action Reviews'. They serve as measuring sticks of where you are and help leaders and units improve their performance. AARs can be either formal or informal. Formal AARs are typically held at the company level and above, although they might also be conducted for small unit gunnery or situational platoon training exercises. Informal AARs are usually conducted at the platoon level and below. These can be done at any time during any training, and they have the advantage of giving soldiers and units immediate feedback.

I mentioned the National Training Center (NTC) in California earlier. It is a model for conducting effective AARs. Located at Fort

Irwin, it serves as one of the Army's premier training locations. It consists of over 1,000 square miles of training ranges and is often referred to in the Army as "the box." It is a large area that allows for free maneuver, with airspace restricted for military use and uncluttered electromagnetic-spectrum access. Units, usually brigades consisting of about 4,000 to 6,000 soldiers, rotate through NTC and conduct exercises under complex scenarios designed to simulate the battlefield and challenge soldiers and leaders to their fullest. An NTC rotation always includes an AAR. Although weeks in the desert are unpleasant, for many, the AAR is often the most disagreeable part of the rotation. The AAR site is set up like a mobile studio about the size of an 18-wheeler truck with top-notch video technology that allows the training staff and the participating unit to see how the training went.

In general, AARs emphasize achieving Army standards while avoiding lecturing, criticizing, or judging individual soldiers' performance. What really makes AARs at the NTC so painful is the fact that soldiers are usually mentally and physically exhausted when they arrive for the AAR after several weeks in the desert – where they don't sleep much.

When you look around the AAR room at your teammates, everybody looks the same—tired and exhausted, but relieved it's almost over. You might have thought you knew your strengths and weaknesses during the exercise, but now it's time to talk about them publicly. Oh, and by the way, you probably didn't get along well with your "observer controller" – the soldier responsible for testing and evaluating your unit while you're "in the box. "But in spite of the agony of an AAR, it's a productive and valuable process.

Step 8—Retrain

Often, leaders are so focused on just getting through the training that *retraining* is the last thing on their minds. Yet retraining is a critical step in developing leaders and achieving tactical and technical proficiency. Dedicating time to retraining allows even the best units to maintain their strengths, improve their performance, or expand their skills through performing the training under different circumstances, such as at night, with a junior leader in charge, or under other conditions intended to challenge the unit.

The Army's Eight Step Training Model paid big dividends for me when I was a platoon leader in the Army. We were preparing for a major field training exercise and evaluation. This evaluation was a big deal and often determined the future career of a young Army officer, especially company commanders. In addition to my platoon responsibilities, I was responsible for the advance party, which is dispatched ahead of the troops to do reconnaissance. In my case, the advance party had a huge role in securing the training site, establishing a perimeter defense, testing for biological, chemical, and nuclear activities, and establishing communications, including running communication wire and connecting telephones.

Just as important, the advance party was responsible for receiving the main body, which consisted of about 120 soldiers, 60 vehicles, and a host of equipment ranging from generators to large fuel pumps. One of the objectives of the advance party when receiving the main body was to make sure that no vehicle would come to a complete stop when entering the perimeter. This meant we had to have a detailed plan of where each vehicle would go on the perimeter and who was responsible for getting that vehicle there. The advance party was about 25 strong with 15 vehicles.

Months before the exercise, we had trained using the Eight Step Training Model. And at the exercise site, while the soldiers looked like ants scurrying all the over place, they operated with a clear task and purpose in mind. When the main body arrived, my company commander was in awe— *"You all did all of this?"* He was amazed, and so was I.

Takeaways:

*   The Army's Eight-Step model is a proven way to approach training effectively
*   Find a training model appropriate for your organization and employees

CHAPTER 5:

MAKING PEACE WITH YOUR HEADQUARTERS
(They're not your enemy)

I've reprinted below a letter dated August 11, 1812 from the Duke of Wellington to the British National Office in London. At the time, Wellington was serving as a commander of British forces and was engaged in a fierce campaign against Napoleon's Army in Spain and Portugal. The letter was directed to British government authorities in London:

Gentlemen,

Whilst marching from Portugal to a position which commands the approach to Madrid and the French forces, my officers have been diligently complying with your requests which have been sent by H.M. ship from London to Lisbon and thence by dispatch to our headquarters.

We have enumerated our saddles, bridles, tents and tent poles, and all manner of sundry items for which His Majesty's Government holds me accountable. I have dispatched reports on the character, wit, and spleen of every officer. Each item and every farthing has been accounted for, with two regrettable exceptions for which I beg your indulgence.

Unfortunately, the sum of one shilling and nine-pence remains unaccounted for in one infantry battalion's petty cash and there has been a hideous confusion as to the number of jars of raspberry jam issued to one cavalry regiment during a sandstorm in western Spain. This reprehensible carelessness may be related to the pressure of circumstance, since we are at war with France, a fact which may come as a bit of a surprise to you gentlemen in Whitehall.

This brings me to my present purpose, which is to request elucidation of my instructions from His Majesty's Government so that I may better understand why I am dragging an army over these barren plains. I construe that perforce it must be one of two alternative duties, as given below. I shall pursue either one with the best of my ability, but I cannot do both:

1. To train an army of uniformed British clerks in Spain for the benefit of the accountants and copy-boys in London or perchance

2. To see to it that the forces of Napoleon are driven out of Spain.

Your most obedient servant,
Wellington

The authenticity of the letter may be in doubt, but the sentiment certainly rings true. I imagine this neatly sums up the feelings of many who have served "at the front" and been confronted with seemingly endless orders and requests for information from their higher headquarters. After all, There is a good reason why it's called the *chain* of command.

In most organizations, especially large ones like the military or big corporations, layers of management, oversight, coordination, and governance in every imaginable form exist from the bottom to the very top. Getting something—*anything*—staffed, reviewed, pre-approved, post-approved, and actually done can sometimes seem like a monumental climb up an unforgiving mountain with chains tied around your ankles.

Many of you have already spent plenty of time in hierarchical organizations. You've also likely heard, and probably contributed to, the daily criticism aimed at your "higher headquarters," "corporate," "command group," "front office," "head-shed," "top-floor"—or whatever it may be called.

"Where bad ideas are born and good ideas go to die" is among the nicer ways I've heard the typical headquarters described over the years.

At many headquarters, everyone seems to have the power to say no, while few have the authority to say yes. Who doesn't feel just a brief pang of worry when you see an e-mail from your headquarters arrive in your inbox?

Tension between those who work "in the trenches" and those responsible for managing large, diverse organizations is a natural, nearly universal phenomenon that's been around for ages.

Many recent books on management and organizational change include recommendations to reduce levels of management, eliminate unnecessary review and approval processes, and empower those who do the actual work. These are worthwhile objectives. No one wants to work for an organization that uses hierarchy like a straitjacket to limit initiative or constrain people's ability to make decisions quickly.

It's important, however, to recognize the very real value that headquarters staffs and senior leaders with a broader perspective bring to a mission or pursuit of a goal. There are reasons why chains of command and headquarters evolved to begin with. Leading far-flung, complex, global operations with tens of thousands of people, each with their own distinct set of tasks, has never been easy. The fact is that hierarchies, chains of command, and higher headquarters are not going to disappear any time soon, despite the best efforts of organizational and management consultants around the globe to flatten us all. So, it's vital to learn how to operate with a HQ and assist it in doing its job well.

First off, reflexively criticizing your higher HQ (and allowing others to do it in your unit) gradually erodes your ability to effectively execute orders and to accomplish your mission. It's also unprofessional and reduces the trust that must exist between leaders and those they lead. We should also never forget that one day, you will likely be assigned to a higher headquarters yourself. Rather than viewing our headquarters as an organizational anachronism or a necessary hindrance, we should see it as a foundation for getting things done right. Especially if the relationship is characterized by mutual understanding and shared vision.

So, how do we make the relationship between those in the trenches or cubicles and those at the headquarters work smoothly for the benefit of all?

One of the first and most important responsibilities of both military professionals and company managers is to fully understand their leadership's *vision, mission, intent, priorities, and guidance.* Sounds simple enough, right? Vision and mission statements are so common today that every organization larger than a lemonade stand has one.

In reality, understanding them requires a lot more than just skimming through them the week you check in for your tour of duty or start your employment. To do your job well and to smoothly lead your unit in support of your organization's objectives, you not only have to read these documents – you need to set aside quiet time to thoroughly think through their implications and the effect they have on your part of your organization's broader mission.

You need to ask yourself questions like, "What are the implied or unstated tasks I need to perform in order to support the commander's or boss's vision and accomplish the mission?"

No mission statement is ever comprehensive enough to answer all your questions or to account for the nearly infinite number of contingencies that will arise. It's therefore your responsibility to analyze the vision and mission of your higher headquarters and understand how your unit helps support them. Doing this requires that you speak to your fellow commanders or managers, staff officers, predecessors, and those currently in your unit to gain the background and context needed to support your headquarters.

From my observation, many subordinate commanders and staffs give short shrift to this effort. They either assume too quickly that they understand the commander's intent without sufficient reflection, or they believe that these documents are minimally relevant to their own day-to-day mission. Not expending enough time and effort to understand your higher headquarters' guidance is a poor idea and leads to misunderstandings, miscommunication, and sub-optimal performance.

Understanding your HQ is just the *first* step, however. What often separates those who excel at command and staff operations from those who merely *perform* them is to *anticipate* what their headquarters will need—before they ask for it (Remember just a few pages ago, that 'anticipation' is one of the critical traits of a good logistician and leader).

Subordinate commanders and staffs who anticipate HQ requirements are worth their weight in gold. And not just because they can "keep the HQ happy." Their true value comes from looking ahead at the operational environment across their entire organization, understanding how they fit within it, and determining what their headquarters will likely need to succeed. True anticipation requires a unit to get inside the *decision cycle* of their HQ so they can shape, influence, and guide the larger organization along the best and most productive path.

Having served and led at several large organizations and with complex staffs, I can attest to the fact that most subordinate commands don't get inside their HQ's or corporate's decision cycle, and so they find themselves reacting to events that appear beyond their control. They feel unable to influence their HQ's decisions.

Here's one example. While serving as the commanding general of the Army's Combined Arms Support Command (CASCOM) in Fort Lee, Virginia, I attended a series of quarterly meetings with my own higher headquarters at the time, the U.S. Army Training and Doctrine Command (TRADOC), a four-star-level organization. It oversees 32 Army schools organized under eight Centers of Excellence, each focused on a separate area of expertise within the Army (such as logistics, maneuver, and signal). These centers train over 500,000 soldiers and other service members each year. In addition, TRADOC is responsible for developing the doctrine that guides how the Army conducts operations. Believe me, within the universe of the Army, TRADOC has a large and critical mission.

However, during these quarterly two-day sessions, led by my four-star commander and attended by my fellow two- and three-star colleagues, it was apparent that while CASCOM was "present and accounted for," we were not influential players and not part of TRADOC's decision cycle. Just showing up, listening, and answering questions when asked isn't good enough. You've got to come prepared to meetings like these ready to actively engage, drive the discussion, and add value to your HQ.

We weren't as ready as we should be, because we lacked an adequate understanding of TRADOC's objectives and priorities. Why was that?

There are many reasons, including the fact that our Army was at war in both Afghanistan and Iraq, while at the same time planning to transition our forces out of those countries. We were also supporting other Army forces deployed all over the world. The sheer operational tempo – or 'OPTEMPO' was incredible (i.e. we were really busy).

We hadn't had the time to fully understand the TRADOC commander's guidance, intent and priorities, and we weren't inside TRADOC's decision cycle. We may have thought we understood these things, but we were fooling ourselves, and it showed during these critical sessions where the HQ was seeking input from us and making decisions about the future of the Army.

So, what did we do about it? We took the TRADOC commander's intent and priorities back to the CASCOM leaders and staff. Then, we did the detailed, painstaking work of figuring out how we fit in, and how we were (*or weren't*) doing our part to support what the higher HQ's commander told us was most important. We next took a step back and figured out how we could better engage during these quarterly sessions—not just to demonstrate that we were in sync with our HQ's priorities, but to go a step further and show how we were *anticipating* where CASCOM and TRADOC needed to go and what we were doing to get us there. Our goal was to use these sessions to help *drive* the larger organization rather than merely coming along for the ride. Only then, could we add value to the higher headquarters.

To maximize our impact at these sessions, our CASCOM staff had to understand what decisions were going to be made at TRADOC's level and get our recommendations to the HQ early on in the decision-making process as the discussions were taking shape. For a subordinate commander, there is just no substitute for making sure (*forcing where necessary*) that your staff engages with their counterparts in the higher HQ. Understanding what topics are ongoing, what policies and programs are in development, and what missions are being planned at the HQ, are part of your staff's daily responsibilities. If you want to have a dog in the fight—much less one that is prepared to win—you've got to understand the *who, what, where,* and *when* of your higher HQ's decision-making process. Simply put, to influence an outcome, you've got to do your homework, and your staff has to stay in constant contact with your HQ.

Every brand-new private in the Army is required during basic training to memorize their chain of command, all the way from the name and rank of their immediate drill sergeant to the president of the United States. The military does this both for practical and cultural reasons.

In a hierarchical organization, people need to know where their orders are going to come from and who they need to answer to. And memorizing the chain of command instills a broad cultural understanding in the military that *everybody*, no matter how senior a general or admiral, has a boss.

As a memory task in boot camp, or when depicted on an organization chart with neat boxes and lines, the chain of command can appear pretty simple and clear-cut. And, for a new private, it pretty much is. However, the higher that individual rises within a chain of command, the more complex the relationships become. The reality is far more nuanced than it appears on a chart. Still, there is no substitute for understanding—and ensuring that everyone you lead also understands—where your unit or staff falls in the organization. You need to know not only who your boss is, and who your boss's boss is, but what organizations are on your left and right and what staff functions will guide and influence the accomplishment of your unit's mission.

One of the most important aspects of both running a military command and successfully engaging with a higher headquarters is understanding how information flows up, down, and across the chain of command. Ensuring that information gets to the right people at the right time, and in an understandable fashion so that decisions can be made, is among the most important responsibilities of any staff member – especially a logistician. The tools for orchestrating this flow of information can sometimes resemble how a symphony, with over 150 musicians playing different instruments, can create a single harmonious piece of music.

In the military, we have adopted a term for this information management and decision-making process called the *battle rhythm*. I don't believe it's an accident that we use the word *rhythm*, which is associated with music. Because establishing the right *battle rhythm* ensures that we gather the right information and get it to the right people just as if we were all musicians playing the same song.

The battle rhythm is usually comprised of a series of briefings, meetings, reports, summaries, recommendations, orders, guidance, policies, information papers, and other products carefully timed to share information and to impose structure and predictability on what can be a very chaotic environment. It can be particularly chaotic during a crisis or other fast-moving event. These briefings and meetings will often have a standard roster of attendees, sequence of events, formats, and deadlines for submitting information and discussion topics. Learning what these are—and making sure your unit adheres to them—is a critical responsibility for any military professional. Even more importantly, there will likely be a set of unwritten and unstated expectations for these briefings and staff documents that you will need to understand and be prepared to meet.

In a military organization, types of meetings and briefings include Commander's Update Briefs (CUB), Battle Update Briefs (BUB), Course of Action (COA) Briefs (intended to convey options for accomplishing a mission or executing a program), Staff Updates, Commander's Updates, Morning "Stand-Up" meetings (usually with the commander and key staff only), Weekly Staff meetings (usually with the commander and the entire staff), In-Progress Reviews (IPRs – meant to update a commander and key staff on a particular mission, event, or program), Decision Briefs (intended to conclude with a formal decision from the commander), and SPOT Reports (used to quickly convey information having an immediate impact on a unit's operations).

Common types of written documents you'll encounter in a HQ include Orders, Fragmentary Orders, Executive Summaries, Situation Reports, Serious Incident Reports, Policies, and Directives.

Whatever the types of meetings, briefings, and documents that are part of your organization's battle rhythm, if it's done right, with the appropriate integration of information in pursuit of common goals, you'll be better able to make sound, timely decisions.

Moral and physical courage, integrity, firmness, fairness, and the ability to inspire confidence in others are some of the key qualities of a successful military leader and logistician. Like it or not, so is the ability to brief.

The word *brief* is both a noun and verb. It refers to a product and an action. *Briefs* and *briefings* are the blood and oxygen that flow through every military organization, especially a headquarters – little gets accomplished without them. Learning to brief well and to write a good brief are indispensable skills.

Trust me, I have screwed up my share of briefings, both in the preparation and the delivery.

As a logistics planner in the 5th Division at Fort Polk, Louisiana, I was responsible for preparing and presenting a briefing on the logistics involved in a major maneuver exercise. I was very enthusiastic about it. However, despite my preparation, I didn't clearly understand the purpose, intent, and desired outcome of the presentation. So, at the conclusion of my briefing, the division commander, Major General Crouch (clearly disappointed), looked at my boss, the chief logistics officer, Colonel McManus (*who was known as 'Hamp'*) and said, "Hamp, you know what we're looking for." That is actually a pretty mild rebuke. But I knew that I had messed up the briefing and that this was only a nice way of telling my boss to fix it. I learned that understanding the purpose of a briefing and the desired result is critical. I also learned that the background and context of the material shape a good brief, and that, if done right, your briefing turns into action. It gets things done.

I have sat in thousands of briefings, and prepared hundreds of others. The quality of a brief and the skill of a briefer often determines the success or failure of a proposal or operation. Briefs in the Army are usually done using PowerPoint slides. There are few things soldiers complain about more than PowerPoint. As a communication medium, it has its limitations. However, its shortcomings are mainly the result of not using PowerPoint creatively or efficiently. For those who dislike PowerPoint, get over it. It's not going away any time soon.

One of the longest evenings of my life was spent preparing a briefing using PowerPoint. I can still vividly remember it. It involved the Army truck strategy I mentioned earlier. The next day we would be briefing senior military leaders and defense industry representatives on a new strategy for the Army. Dozens of highly experienced officers, NCOs, and subject matter experts (SMEs) had been working on the strategy for many months. The decisions we made about the future of the Army's vehicle fleet would have consequences measured in hundreds of millions of dollars and in jobs for tens of thousands of defense industry workers. The success or failure of numerous acquisition programs involving dozens of major defense contractors was also at stake. Most importantly, so was the ability of the Army and our sister services to fight and maneuver on future battlefields. And I was feeling the pressure.

By the evening, the PowerPoint slides used to depict our proposed truck strategy had already gone through countless versions and revisions. However, the brief still needed work. As we were less than 24 hours from presenting it to the senior military leaders and defense industry reps, we were feeling both the press of time and the stress of trying to present the strategy in a way that a diverse audience with different and conflicting interests would understand and support.

To finalize the brief, Lieutenant General Benjamin Griffin (who I mentioned earlier as well, and was a great leader and skilled briefer) and I locked ourselves in a hotel room to make the final tweaks. At one point, LTG Griffin looked at me and said, "We'll do this together and work it until we get it right!" He understood that by this stage, the staffs and SMEs had done their jobs and that the brief now needed to be honed one-on-one.

LTG Griffin also understood that not only did every word, image, statistic, and recommendation on the slides have to be right, we had to account for the unique interests of every party involved.

Given what was at stake, we knew that our brief would be challenged and second-guessed by everyone from CEOs to our fellow generals and members of Congress and their staffs.

After two and half hours of poring over those PowerPoint slides, LTG Griffin flipped his eyeglasses onto his forehead, peered at me, and said, "Larry, you probably feel like jumping out of that 4th floor window."

I looked back at him and replied, "Yes, sir, I do."

"Larry, just remember I'll be there to catch you," he responded.

To this day, I reflect on that experience. "I'd rather be back in Afghanistan than have to do another briefing like that," I've even remarked. But the episode taught me the importance of being fully prepared when giving a presentation. Just as importantly, I learned it's a godsend to have a boss who is tough, caring, and knows how to give a brief.

Takeaways:

* Your headquarters (HQ) is not your enemy
* Understand your HQs decision cycle & influence it
* Pay attention to the flow of information to and from your HQ
* The ability to brief is key to your – and your command's – success

Corpus Christi State University circa May 1982, my Second Lieutenant commissioning with Denise and Edith, my Mother.

August 1988 CPT Wyche and Denise.

July 2010, throwing the first pitch at the Houston Astros vs. Pittsburgh Pirates baseball game at Minute Maid Park. Lucky for me I threw a strike!

Paul Cameron, college professor, mentor and friend.

*November 2015, enjoying the kids at Whitesburg
Elementary School in Huntsville, Alabama*

*July 1994 at Fort Polk, Louisiana, Lieutenant Colonel Sumpter and Denise
pinning on my major rank with daughters Tori and Meagan*

*June 2012 Fort Lee, Virginia, assuming command
of the Combined Arms Support Command*

*Rock Island, Illinois August 2008, General Griffin, son David, First
Lieutenant at my promotion ceremony to Brigadier General*

CHAPTER 6:

SEEING THE BATTLEFIELD FROM END TO END

(Supply Chain Training for Afghanistan)

We were about eight months into our Afghanistan deployment and sitting in what we called the "Skinner Inn," an
old building made from plywood that the senior noncommissioned
and junior officers fixed up so that they would have somewhere to
go and relax, drink some pop (no alcohol in Afghanistan), and tell
stories during the very little time off we had.

It was a Friday evening, and on Fridays, 10 to 20 Muleskinner
leaders (*'Muleskinner' was the nickname for our unit*) would meet
at the dining hall for dinner. We all enjoyed dining on Friday, because it was seafood night. Also, for me, that was the one day that I
treated myself to desert. You named it, the dining hall had it, from
chocolate cake, ice cream of all types, and other treats.

These Friday evenings were important for many reasons. One is
we could talk candidly, which was important to me as the brigade

commander because it was an opportunity to show the brigade leaders that I would listen to them. Of course, I had to be ready to handle the good, the bad, and the ugly of what the team would tell me.

Well, this one particular Friday evening, Staff Sergeant Major Tom Stiefermann and I were chatting. "Sir, I have to tell you," he said, "while preparing for our deployment, I—and many others— thought you had lost a screw or two by having us go through that ridiculous supply chain class and supply chain certification program."

Truth be told, the idea for the supply chain certification training came from my deputy, Lieutenant Colonel Bob Gagnon, who was an exceptional soldier, logistician, and experienced warfighter, having been deployed several times. Prior to our deployment to Afghanistan, each NCO and officer who worked in the brigade headquarters had to be supply-chain certified on their class of supply (such as food and water, munitions, repair parts, and fuel, to name just a few). Which meant they needed to learn how their supply class moved from the manufacturer to the Army depot in the U.S. to the port and then across the globe to a forward operating base in Afghanistan.

Lieutenant Colonel Gagnon's idea proved critical to the brigade's mission because forcing our soldiers to learn the entire supply chain from end to end for each item bridged critical gaps in their knowledge. The training allowed them to move back and forth from the little details (i.e. logistics operations in Afghanistan) to the big picture (i.e. the complex supply chain that manufactured, distributed, and repaired our equipment all across the globe).

For example, ammunition is a critical supply class, and we had to understand hundreds of different variables to ensure that the right ammo got to the right unit on time. We had to continually ask ourselves, "What are the requirements for that type of ammunition? Where is that ammunition coming from in the U.S.? When is it supposed to be in Afghanistan? And, how do we move it in-country?"

The supply chain certification training produced several outcomes in addition to teaching the trainees the importance of seeing the logistics battlefield from end to end, as we put it. It taught us how to determine where the supply item was in the pipeline at any given time. It also taught us how to identify where the 'choke points' were in the pipeline. The places where the flow of an item was most likely to be constricted or stopped. That was absolutely critical. In those cases where we might not be able to eliminate the choke point, it allowed us to predict and manage how to respond if a supply item got stuck somewhere in the supply chain. I would often ask my team, "If you know you are about to get hit on the head with a baseball bat, what are you going to do? Put on a helmet? Duck? Take cover?" My point was that you would protect yourself. We knew that if we protected our logistics operations by managing the choke points and problem areas in the pipeline, clearly we'd be more successful.

In the case of ammunition, the supply chain training helped us identify seven choke points and develop mitigation strategies to combat every one of these problem areas. For each choke point, we knew the points of contact (who to call and what to say), whether at sea, at the port, in another country such as Germany, or in the air. As a result of their training, our youngest NCOs and officers found themselves briefing senior leaders with the tremendous confidence. Many of these individuals worked for Staff Sergeant Major Stiefermann, and he could not have been prouder of each of them.

The corporate world is really no different when it comes to supply chains. You need to see the pipeline from end to end, learn the entire chain for each item, and understand all the different variables involved to ensure the right supplies are delivered in the right quantities at the right time. Proper supply chain training is key.

I remember arriving at Bagram airfield in Afghanistan in February 2006. I was a colonel with nearly three decades of service in the Army. I had been a logistician for 24 years, served in a wide variety of assignments, commanded a company and a battalion, and served at the Pentagon. I had been to several excellent military schools. Like many others in my position, being a young colonel, I was pretty good at tactical logistics, and to some, degree operational logistics. However, I didn't fully understand the capabilities and limitations of key organizations assigned to the larger Joint Logistics Command that I now led. Despite the excellent supply chain training we gave to our soldiers and young officers, I quickly came to realize I still didn't have the detailed knowledge to reach back to the defense industrial base back in the United States and all around the world. As I stepped off the aircraft and assumed responsibility for supporting the logistics of all joint forces in Afghanistan, I suspected I would encounter gaps in my knowledge and holes in my experience.

Boy, was I right.

Despite the training I'd been given, I didn't fully understand logistics in a combat environment as complex and difficult as Afghanistan, much less an environment that contained more than two dozen coalition partners, thousands of members of the inter-agency community, tens of thousands of contract personnel, and supply lines that traversed some of the most geographically demanding and politically hostile territory in the world.

As an example, one day, a team of twelve people from the Defense Logistics Agency (DLA) arrived at my headquarters and informed me that they were there to join my team. I didn't have any idea how I would use them. Some prior, well-thought-out planning about their availability and use would have been beneficial. Ultimately, they became my link to consumable supplies in nine different supply chains emanating from the Defense Department and commercial industry in the United States and throughout the rest of the world. This DLA link ultimately proved vital to getting our warfighters what they needed.

Afghanistan presented endless logistics challenges, although our biggest one was distribution. There were problems getting supplies via Pakistan, and via the northern distribution route through Europe. Afghanistan had only one functioning airport. Transporting supplies within Afghanistan was also a nightmare. At the time, Afghanistan had only 2,800 kilometers (1,739 miles) of paved roads. Alternate routes were often unfeasible because of the terrain, which ranged from rugged mountains to deserts. Beside the primitive road system, there were no formal communication networks. On top of all that, there was Afghanistan's severe climate. On a single day alone, we experienced snow in the northeast, a wind storm in the central region, and arid desert temperatures in southwest Afghanistan. Anticipating the weather and its impact on when we could fly was essential. When the window was open, we had better be in the air.

Most importantly, there were enemy forces and IEDs (improvised explosive devices) to contend with. A senior Army leader, Lieutenant General Christianson, later commented that, if someone had said before the U.S. entered Afghanistan, "In the next fight we're going to have to move fuel 1,600 miles through enemy territory, negotiate mountain passes that are sometimes closed in the winter, and deliver that fuel to ground forces that will be distributed in forward operating bases that are disconnected in a country with an unreliable road network—and we will sustain that operation for three or four years"—other people "would have thought you were crazy. They would have told you that you couldn't do it."

In 1999, General Eric Shinseki, the new Army Chief of Staff, asked his staff to put a map above his desk of the most uninviting and inauspicious place the Army could conduct military operations. His staff hung a map of Afghanistan.[4]

To combat these distribution challenges, we used a combination of transport means, ranging from air drops to rotary wing helicopters to fixed wing aircraft to jingle trucks. During 2006–2007, when I was the senior logistician, we conducted over 300 airdrops of more than 3,000 bundles of supplies. Eleven different routes were used by our helicopters to deliver mail, ammunitions, and critical repairs, as well as to transport our soldiers. 'Jingle trucks' *(I'll say more about these in a later chapter, but they are basically small to medium sized, local, commercial trucks driven by our contractor workforce)* played a critical part in our distribution effort; on average, there were 3,000 to 4,500 trucks on the road during a typical month. They suffered well over 100 attacks during the year I was there. But despite the many challenges we faced, I know of no Commander who could not accomplish their mission because they didn't get the supplies they needed.

Although I have tried hard not to micromanage many things in the Army, distribution operations in Afghanistan was one of the few where I did.

Perhaps the biggest lesson I learned as a logistician in Afghanistan was that our institutional training model for logisticians wasn't

---

4   Walker, Afghanistan Expeditionary Sustainment Operations, manuscript draft, Chapter One, "Evolution of Sustainment and Support Doctrine and Systems, 1990–2001," p. 46; Chapter Two, "Overview of Sustainment Operations in Theater during Operation Enduring Freedom, 2001–2014," pp. 1-5.

right. I've already mentioned just a few of the areas where we didn't fully understand some critical part of logistics at the strategic level and the global supply chain. So, I made a promise with myself while deployed that if I ever was in a position to affect how the Army and DoD train our logisticians, I would.

Fast forward six years from our time in Afghanistan. I was now serving as the Commanding General of the Army's Combined Arms Support Command (CASCOM), which was responsible for training over a hundred thousand Army logisticians and sustainers and developing future logistics doctrine. I managed an operating budget of $215 million. At CASCOM, we spent a great deal of time discussing and debating how we should train the future logistics force and develop leaders. Our discussions resulted in a detailed document: "Army 2020 and Beyond Sustainment White Paper."[5]

In the white paper, we described the implications for Army sustainment (which consists of logistics, personnel services, and health service support) posed by future strategic environments requiring us to execute a range of very different missions – all simultaneously. We pointed out that these environments will likely differ from the wars in Afghanistan and Iraq, and that the United States would probably have to focus on the Asia-Pacific and Europe regions.

5   Walker, Afghanistan Expeditionary Sustainment Operations, manuscript draft, Chapter One, "Evolution of Sustainment and Support Doctrine and Systems, 1990–2001," p. 46; Chapter Two, "Overview of Sustainment Operations in Theater during Operation Enduring Freedom, 2001–2014," pp. 1-5.

We predicted logisticians would encounter "a variety of conflicts between rapidly evolving and adaptive threats," including conventional forces, irregular militias, cyber attackers, terrorist groups, and non-state actors. "The proliferation of weapons of mass destruction adds an even more deadly complication to the environments where the Army will potentially have to operate," we noted. And "our end state must be a sustainment system that is lean, yet flexible, [and] adaptive enough to expand to meet future operational requirements."

The CASCOM team argued that the force structure and equipment of sustainment units should be focused on building "the necessary protection, mobility, firepower, and communications" that would support what we called 'decisive action' against this range of threats. Sustainment leaders must be trained, and able to execute, differing sustainment missions simultaneously, we stressed. In addition to decisive action against this variety of threats, such missions might also include building partner capacity (i.e. training other nation's Army and military forces), humanitarian assistance, and disaster relief. "When this training, education, and experience in sustainment leaders is matched with world class organizational structures and equipment," we wrote, "sustainment organizations will be able to readily adapt to a range of missions."

We asserted that sustainment operations had to execute nine key sustainment tasks in the future strategic environment, ranging from shaping operations and maintaining readiness to organizing theater drawdowns and reconstituting forces. Plus, the future sustainment force needed to be integrated with a range of partners, self-protected, precise, and responsive to Army needs.

Our conclusions highlighted two critical areas:

Leader Attributes

We reached the conclusion that effectively operating in the future strategic environment as part of a multinational force with limited resources would require a "new set of skills for sustainment leaders." They "must be adaptive professionals who can think critically to solve problems as they support multiple mission types concurrently and adjust to evolving circumstances,." And they "must be able to plan and execute sustainment from the tactical through the strategic levels," while balancing the diverse interests of partner organizations. They had to be skilled at getting results through cooperative arrangements. In addition, they required "expertise in defense industrial base management and total life cycle systems management [of weapons] as well as sustainment planning and supply chain management across all levels." If that sounds familiar to earlier parts of the book, it's no coincidence.

Training

We also argued it was essential that current training for sustainment leaders replicate the future operational environment as much as possible. Further, "as a part of the training effort," we wrote, "we must leverage technology whenever it is feasible, realistic, and affordable. Simulations and gaming solutions can be used to develop and maintain perishable skills in varied and challenging conditions."

To ensure challenging and realistic training, we noted, it was especially important that there be "command post exercises, functional training, and combat training center rotations that force sustainment leaders to adapt to a diverse set of circumstances." The leaders must "proactively embrace these readiness exercises as a means of testing sustainment and developing and maintaining critical skills. These and other exercises must be designed to physically and intellectually test the participants."

Our team also stressed that the education of sustainment leaders had to include not only comprehensive professional military education, but "other educational opportunities, such as advanced civilian schooling and Army partnerships with civilian educational institutions." Finally, we advised that future leaders be identified earlier in their careers so that their training and education would provide them with an even stronger foundation of knowledge about sustainment and all that it required.

The white paper was a lot to take in. But the challenges the Army faced in the future strategic environment were great, and a lot was at stake. We hoped our paper would stimulate more ideas about how our Army should sustain itself in the next war and how we train our logisticians. And in that, I believe it succeeded.

Takeaways:

* See the supply chain pipeline from end to end
* Anticipate & identify supply chain shortfalls and choke points
* Develop mitigating strategies that address shortfalls and choke points
* Developing your supply chain leaders is essential

CHAPTER 7:

AMERICA'S MILITARY INSURANCE POLICY
(The Organic Industrial Base)

A s I mentioned earlier, even after serving in the Army for over twenty years, I still didn't fully understand something the Department of Defense calls its *"Organic Industrial Base."* Parts of which I've already eluded to.

After all, I was getting the equipment and the material we needed to support our organizations and formations from "the system." I never really stopped and pondered what that system was. As a military logistician, however, knowledge of the *Organic Industrial Base* is more critical than ever.

Equipment does not magically fall out of the sky.

At the heart of "the system" is the *Organic Industrial Base (or OIB)* and all of the processes that bring items into that 'base' for repair, rebuild or recapitalization, and then out to the warfighter. If your goal is to be a well-rounded military logistician and to truly understand supply chain operations, you have to understand the industrial base that supports your operations. The same is likely true for logisticians in the corporate world: you need to know all about the 'base' that produces the parts and products you need.

For many years, and for all the right reasons, my focus was on tactical and operational logistics, and I always wanted to serve in the Army's Divisions and Corps. After all, that's where the action is. But there is also lots of exciting action in the OIB.

The Army's Organic Industrial Base refers to all of the Army's government-owned maintenance depots, manufacturing facilities, and ammunition plants. The OIB performs a wide range of activities, from repairing broken equipment to refurbishing weapons systems and extending their useful life. It also upgrades and modernizes major weapons systems and platforms – not just making them like new but incorporating updated technology to make them better and more reliable. And it manufactures lots of weapons and equipment. From rebuilding tanks, trucks, and helicopters, to manufacturing hundreds of thousands of 9-millimeter rounds and large bombs (such as 5,000-pounders), it accomplishes a huge range of complex and essential tasks.

The OIB is the foundation of our system for keeping the military's vast array of equipment maintained and up-to-date and ensuring that our armed forces have the materiel resources needed to accomplish a variety of missions. It exists to preserve America's core military capabilities and is necessary to fulfill both strategic and contingency plans. Because many of its facilities, equipment, capabilities, and skilled personnel are unique to the OIB, it also serves as the nation's 'insurance policy' by making sure we will have critical repair facilities ready when we need them. It also ensures we have the trained people needed to perform distinct, unique military logistics tasks. These highly-trained professionals often cannot be found in the private sector. (It isn't always cost-effective or competitive for private companies, even big ones in the defense industry, to maintain these very niche capabilities and skills.)

As a result, the OIB is both invaluable and irreplaceable. Yet, many people have never heard of it, as it draws little public or media attention.

Each of the military services—the Army, Navy, Marine Corps, and Air Force—operate and maintain maintenance depots and repair facilities for their own equipment and weapon systems. The Army's OIB consists of a number of major commands and subordinate units. These include four "lifecycle management" commands—the Tank-Automotive and Armaments Command, Communications-Electronics Command, Aviation and Missile Command, and Joint Munitions and Lethality Command, which are the heart of the Army's industrial base capabilities. They are called "lifecycle" commands because they support Army equipment requirements throughout each item's lifecycle. This means from the moment the item is delivered to the Army for use; then during the many years soldiers employ it; until it is no longer needed and is either sold, discarded, or otherwise removed from the force.

Today, the Army's Organic Industrial Base, under the management of the U.S. Army Materiel Command, consists of 23 unique, one-of-a-kind industrial facilities: three manufacturing arsenals, nine repair and overhaul depots, and 11 ammunition plants. These facilities manufacture everything from bullets to cannons to bombs. The OIB is the only source for certain levels of repair to tank engines, helicopters, and military ambulances. It's the only source for some weapons like mortars and artillery tubes. For example, Watervliet Arsenal in rural New York may be the only manufacturer of cannon tubes left in the Western Hemisphere. Parts of the OIB are virtually the only reliable producers and suppliers of critical materials in North America. Every day, the OIB quietly, in the background, rebuilds hundreds of helicopters, trucks, tanks, and communications equipment.

For much of the past two decades, the Army's depots and arsenals were in overdrive to support the wars in Afghanistan and Iraq while simultaneously supporting the global sustainment operations of a military with personnel and units on every continent. They produced, for example, thousands of mortar systems and hundreds of thousands of critical repair parts and reset (i.e. returned to their optimal condition following aging and the stress of use) millions of pieces of equipment. During 2014 alone, the Army's depots repaired over 110,000 pieces of equipment.

With the drawdown in troops and equipment from Afghanistan and Iraq, the Army had to invest over $30 billion to reset 3.9 million equipment items. It repaired, refurbished, recapitalized, or redistributed some 24,000 armored and wheeled vehicles (if lined up in a convoy, it would stretch almost the entire length of the east coast); over 7,000 mine-resistant ambush protected vehicles (a convoy of 'MRAPs' alone would run from Boston to Washington, D.C.); over 1,000 pieces of road-clearing equipment (more than enough to handle a winter snowstorm in New York State); some 850 helicopters and other aircraft (in September 2014, FedEx reported that it conducted worldwide operations with a fleet of 656 aircraft); and over two million pieces of other equipment, including forklifts, trucks, generators, and fuel tanks.

The OIB is a multi-billion-dollar annual operation that employs thousands of government civilians, military personnel, and contractors. During the wars in Afghanistan and Iraq, the OIB's workload rose from 12.5 million depot labor hours in 2003 to a peak of 29.9 million hours in 2008. If measured in corporate terms, the size and budget of the U.S. Army Materiel Command would rank it along with many in the Fortune 500.

Since I had the opportunity to manage the operations of the Joint Munitions Command, I have seen up close what the OIB does and how it plays a quiet but irreplaceable role in maintaining our national military strength.

The Paladin Howitzer

Take the case of the M109A6 and AZ Paladin howitzer. Many reading this book won't even know what that is. But the M109 has been a mainstay of the Army's artillery since the Vietnam War in the 1960s–1970s (it was later used in the Gulf War, Somalia, Bosnia, Iraq and Afghanistan). It is the Army's primary self-propelled howitzer, and the special skills and capabilities in the Organic Industrial Base are essential to its production.

In late 2010, the program management of the Army's Heavy Brigade Combat Team was preparing the howitzer for the new Paladin Integrated Management Program (PIM) – an upgrade to the system. As the program management team was conducting preliminary inspections of the Paladin howitzer's cannon tubes, they discovered that the bore evacuators on the tubes were corroded.

Why is that a problem? Well, when the howitzer is fired, the bore evacuators prevent the gasses that propel the projectile out of the tube from leaking until it has cleared the barrel. The bore evacuator seals have to open at just the right moment to allow the gasses to escape so they don't go back into the turret and suffocate the crew of the vehicle on which the howitzer is mounted. The bore evacuators consist of a series of precisely drilled holes with seals and bearings. Since many of our howitzers hadn't been used as much as they had in the past, they had spent more time in storage. And during that storage, moisture had seeped into the bore evacuators, causing corrosion around the holes.

The program management of the Heavy Brigade Combat Team brought this problem to the attention of Benet Laboratories, which is part of the Army's Weapons and Software Engineering Center at the Watervliet Arsenal. Working closely with other Army experts, including at the Tank-Automotive and Armaments Command (headquartered outside of Detroit, Michigan), the Benet and Watervliet teams found that nearly 75 percent of the Paladin howitzers in the Army's inventory had corrosion problems. The corrosion significantly increased the wear on the barrel and rendered use of the howitzers unsafe. They were not fit to be deployed on the battlefield. This was a gargantuan problem: an Army without a sufficient number of self-propelled howitzers is a weakened Army. The shortfall could be exploited by the enemy. A simple matter of corrosion had reduced our Army's combat readiness.

Personnel from Benet Labs visited the Anniston Army Depot (located in Anniston, Alabama) to collect data and assess the condition of the cannon barrels and the extent of the damage. The experts involved applied their unique skills to engineer a temporary repair procedure for those barrels that could be repaired and a plan for replacing barrels that couldn't be fixed. Ultimately, Watervliet Arsenal completed temporary repairs on many barrels and replaced most that could not be fixed. And, in 2015, the Army rolled out the new Paladin PIM, which, among other improvements to the previous model, put the howitzer tube on a dramatically redesigned platform, effectively installing the old gun turret on a new chassis.

The unique capabilities required to do all this do not exist in the commercial sector. The only place the Army could turn to for this kind of rapid analysis and repair, and the design and production of a whole new howitzer, was its Organic Industrial Base, a real example of how the OIB really is the nation's insurance policy.

Preserving the Organic Industrial Base

A key requirement for maintaining the U.S. capacity to wage and sustain campaigns in multiple theaters at once and a range of missions is a strong OIB. To remain agile, flexible, and efficient while attentive to costs, senior logisticians must reengineer industrial and sustainment operations – beginning with the OIB in mind. The Army has been transforming its OIB by using new, more cost-effective, and efficient systems for managing its supply chain operations. It has also eliminated many obsolete OIB facilities, cut energy costs, decreased the number of worker accidents (by around 20 percent, with millions of dollars in savings in workers compensation), and reduced lost labor time due to illness or injury.

In 2012, the Army released its "Organic industrial Base Strategic Plan 2012–2022."[6] This detailed document outlined a strategy to ensure that the AOIB remained viable, effective, and efficient, and able to meet future contingency requirements. It included a number of initiatives that were undertaken under the management of the Army Materiel Command (AMC), Assistant Secretary of Army Acquisition Logistics and Technology and key stakeholders, including:

✓ Balancing industrial capacity: The Army and AMC reviewed critical industrial base skills and capabilities against anticipated future requirements to align infrastructure and the workforce

---

6 The plan's full text is available at: https://www.army.mil/e2/c/downloads/276549.pdf

with declining demand given U.S. troop withdrawals in Afghanistan and Iraq. Cutting the OIB's workforce while maintaining essential skills remains one of our most difficult tasks.

✓ Investing in the preservation of critical capabilities: AMC invested over $1 billion in equipment and infrastructure in one six-year period. Projections also called for an annual investment of several million in military construction for the following 15 years to upgrade important facilities and infrastructure.

✓ Aligning resources: OIB operations that had similar capabilities or lacked sufficient workloads were consolidated.

✓ Leveraging commercial capabilities: AMC reached out to commercial manufacturers to identify areas where the capabilities of both could be exploited. Through the Public-Private Partnership Program, investment sharing and collaboration helped optimize capability. In the fiscal year 2015, AMC had well over 200 active partnerships with private-sector companies that generated millions in revenue.

✓ Contracting: AMC used contracting as a tool to increase efficiencies and leverage resources. Several of the OIB's ammunition plants are now operated by private-sector firms under facilities-use contracts. At AMC's Lake City, Missouri ammunition plant, contractor efficiencies are estimated to save millions over the life of the contract.

✓ Reaching out to small businesses: This optimizes the supply chain and helps meet regulatory requirements. On average, over $8 billion has been invested by the Army via AMC in small businesses annually in recent years. As my old boss, General

Dennis Via would often say, "small business is really big business" for America, the Army, and AMC.

✓ Continuous process improvement: AMC is committed to embedding a culture of stewardship and efficiency across the organization. The OIB adopted Lean Six Sigma, a method for boosting performance and reducing costs by eliminating waste, resulting in reduced repair times, greater equipment readiness, and lower production costs.

Still, it will be a challenge to maintain a strong Organic Industrial Base. The OIB depends on government appropriations to deliver materiel readiness. But as with any other insurance policy, it is tempting to stop paying the premiums when the money can be used elsewhere. And, given our fiscal reality, that temptation can be strong.

In March of 2017, as deputy commanding general of the AMC, I testified before the Readiness Subcommittee of the Senate Armed Services Committee on the importance of adequately funding the OIB. "Now more than ever, we must enhance our readiness through continued investment in our organic capabilities," I stressed. "And a foundation of Army readiness is a vibrant and responsive industrial base. We cannot afford to let our warfighting capabilities fall into decay, because within the OIB resides one-of-a-kind resources that cannot be easily revived or replicated, and certainly not in time to respond to a national crisis."

If we do not sufficiently fund the OIB, the effects will also spill over into the commercial sector. Some 75 percent of the nation's broader defense industrial base resides there, and if no demand or orders are forthcoming, companies will seek other business opportunities. That's understandable; thus, the challenge will be to maintain a strong and responsive industrial capability when demand is significantly lower.

We must also recruit the most talented people to ensure that the OIB remains a modern enterprise that meets both wartime and peacetime needs. That, too, will require sufficient investment.

If we allow the OIB to erode over time, we will lose one of the most important, yet often overlooked, foundations of America's military strength. As logisticians, we play a key role in ensuring the role of the OIB is understood by those responsible for making national security funding and policy decisions.

Takeaways:

*   The Organic Industrial Base (OIB) is America's insurance policy
*   Preserving the OIB is essential to maintaining America's military strength
*   Materiel and supplies don't fall out of the sky – know the OIB's capabilities

CHAPTER 8:

ENTERPRISE RESOURCE PLANNING & INTEGRATED LOGISTICS INFORMATION TECHNOLOGY

(Moving From "Blunt Force" Logistics to Precise Support)

There are numerous trends in the world today that require the United States to conduct multiple missions overseas simultaneously. They include the acquisition of advanced technology by terrorists, growing threats posed by non-state actors, erosion of U.S. technological advantages over state competitors (e.g., China, Russia, Iran, and North Korea), and increasing conflict in cyberspace.

The global deployment of logistics assets and a system able to deliver are essential to meet these potential threats. So is national materiel readiness to supply U.S. and allied forces. Army logisticians are central to the U.S. ability to provide this support. Like businesses such as Amazon, Army logisticians have to deliver expeditiously, but they often have to do it under severe, violent, and unpredictable circumstances. The Pacific region, one U.S. focus, is especially demanding, given its vast distances, the length of the supply chain, and the technological and other means of regional states to deny access to U.S. forces.

The European theater also presents formidable challenges. Prior to transitioning out of the Army, I had the opportunity to participate in several logistics reconnaissance surveys in Europe to determine what it would take to support our soldiers should we have to go to war there. A key takeaway from these surveys was that a logistics information system that integrates all aspects of support, one that optimizes reliability and availability, would be essential to that fight.

In the event of a war in Europe, the United States may have to move logistics assets through several countries and a small number of access points, under the threat of air and sea interdiction and long-range precision fires (an DoD term that refers to precise modern missiles capable of striking rapidly from great distances) against land forces. Something as simple as the different sizes of railroad tracks used in European countries also pose a significant obstacle to getting supplies where they have to go. Imagine Amazon needing to deliver packages within 72 hours while the planes, trucks, and delivery drivers are being shot at or hit by missiles!

As part of its efforts to reengineer its industrial and sustainment operations to be more agile, flexible, and efficient, in the 2000s the Army embraced something called 'Enterprise Resource Planning' (or 'ERP')[7]. It is a more effective and economical alternative to the Army's previous approach to supply chain management, which was, in a nutshell, "order, then expedite" without clear priorities, also known as "blunt force" logistics. ERP, uses both computer hardware and software to revolutionize the Army's logistics and supply chain operations. It's a fully integrated system that incorporates suppliers, customers, products, services, processes, the workforce, and other elements of the supply chain.

In the business world, ERP is also used to integrate into a single system the central processes needed to run a company (though the term usually refers specifically to the software). It provides businesses with up-to-the-minute awareness of these processes through a common database and computer system and improves their efficiency. It's so widely used in business today that ERP itself is a huge industry.

People who spend time with me will often hear me say that "we must see ourselves from end to end." This vantage point was critical when it came to distributing material at our ports of embarkation and debarkation. One of the biggest problems we faced in both the Iraq and Afghanistan conflicts, besides those I've already mentioned, was the all-too-common need for soldiers and contractors

---

7   This chapter is based mainly on Larry Wyche's "Delivering Materiel Readiness: From 'Blunt Force' Logistics to Enterprise Resource Planning," Association of the United States Army, June 2016.

to have to sort through myriad pallets of containers and boxes to find that one part needed to support a specific weapons system.

During the earlier Gulf War in 1990–1991, the Army's logistics system relied on gigantic stockpiles of supplies to make up for its inefficiencies; logisticians had problems tracking assets in transit, and military units sometimes couldn't find their supply containers among the masses of containers on U.S. bases.[8] Later, it was a challenge to provide full visibility of critical repair parts that were in the pipeline so that a division commander and other officers could project weapons systems availability, combat power, and overall materiel readiness. Army leaders concluded that the best possible ERP system was a must.

The Army's Logistics Modernization Program (LMP) is a large-scale ERP application of the Army's efforts to overhaul its logistics and supply chain operations.[9] It parallels many practices in the business world. As the name suggests, LMP is designed to modernize supply chain management to more efficiently get equipment and parts to deployed forces around the world. It is designed to streamline supply lines and distribution, decrease operational costs, and integrate in one system all aspects of the supply chain, from

8   Walker, Afghanistan Expeditionary Sustainment Operations, manuscript draft, chapter one, "Evolution of Sustainment and Support Doctrine and Systems, 1990-2001," pp. 7-9.
9   For a concise early account of the benefits of LMP, see Kevin Carroll and David W. Coker, "Logistics Modernization Program: A Cornerstone of Army Transformation," Army Logistician, January–February 2007.

sourcing to delivery. It provides far greater ability to satisfy the Army's many operational needs than earlier systems.

LMP is a critical component of the Army's Single Army Logistics Enterprise (SALE), which was implemented in 2007 and enables across-the-board, A–Z resource planning. SALE allows parties throughout the entire logistics enterprise to access the same data in real time (including the condition of equipment, available materiel and supplies, their location, transit times, and costs). It provides complete asset visibility and accountability. At the time, SALE was one of the largest and most comprehensive logistics system overhauls ever attempted by a government or a business.

Two other elements of SALE are the Global Combat Support System-Army (or 'GCCS-A') and the General Fund Enterprise Business System (or 'GFEBS'). GCCS-A (an acronym pronounced like 'Geeks-Ay') fundamentally changed the Army's supply chain management by integrating several functions into a single system. It is one of the largest ERP's in the Defense Department. GFEBS entails comprehensive financial, asset, and accounting management.

LMP replaced some old and cumbersome Army logistics and supply chain management systems. From 1977 until 2007, the Army relied mainly on the Commodity Command Standard System (CCSS) and the Standard Depot System (SDS). Their programming employed highly intricate processes, and given the complexity of the supporting software and hardware, the Army had to develop a web of "work-around" solutions that ultimately proved inadequate.

The problems with these systems became especially acute in the early 2000s, when the Army lacked available war reserves (material held in storage for use if needed in war) and had to replace outdated weapons systems. Prior to the September 11, 2001 terrorist attacks, Army war reserves were at one of their lowest points in recent history. After September 11, the Army had to fight a war and did not have the luxury to spend time launching a huge effort to create a customized software solution.

However, in the years after September 11th, the need to further integrate the Army's systems for managing its supplies became crystal clear with these mounting requirements. Supporting the materiel requirements of the war and repairing or replacing damaged equipment placed a severe strain on the Army's supply chain. There were duplications, delays, and shortages. Moreover, unscheduled orders sent from other Department of Defense organizations consumed resources earmarked for the Army. To address these and other problems, the Army reached out to civilian IT vendors for commercial off-the-shelf solutions. SAP, an industry leader in ERP, became a key partner in this effort.

The Army wanted to replace CCSS and SDS with a single, comprehensive, and far more efficient logistics and supply management system. LMP integrates more than 80 Defense Department systems and manages billions of dollars of inventory and tens of thousands of vendor transactions. LMP is now employed at numerous industrial sites and has thousands of users. Its functions include ammunition management, depot maintenance planning, inventory management, requisition processing, financial management, services and item procurement, and item introduction and total package fielding. This is an enormously complicated effort in an organization the size of the Army. Among its other benefits, LMP upgrades order fulfillment processes—such as by providing instantaneous information on inventory—improves logistical decision-making and forecasting and provides complete reporting of the costs of goods and services.

The LMP also establishes an important foundation for developing two critical logistical capabilities for the future—the ability to build small, expeditionary manufacturing and fabrication facilities much closer to the battlefield, and the ability to repair, refit, and manufacture critical equipment and weapons on a smaller scale. These capabilities will reduce the length of the Army's supply chain and further decrease costs.

Some Challenges and Lessons of ERP and LMP

As the Army continues to fine-tune its use of Enterprise Resource Planning (including LMP), transitioning from "blunt force" logistics to precise demand forecasting has been challenging. So has creating a culture of collaboration and understanding as people adjust to the new systems. Getting the leadership and the workforce to buy into an ERP program while implementing it can be a daunting task. Frankly, there were Army leaders who believed the investment of resources was not worth the effort. And many members of the Army's workforce were fearful of losing their jobs because of the improvements in efficiency. During the fielding of LMP, we also found many people simply did not want to change— "we never did it that way before." I believe they were afraid to abandon pencil and paper for information technology.

While the employment of LMP immeasurably improved logistics management integration, other critical tasks, such as developing a comprehensive supply chain strategy, required a good deal of further work. So, the Army created a supply chain transformation team within its Organic Industrial Base to address these needs. The team developed and put into practice a comprehensive supply chain strategy across the entire logistics enterprise, one that was enhanced by the implementation of LMP and Complex Assembly Manufacturing Solution (CAMS) software. This strategy strengthened communication throughout the supply chain, thereby improving planning and scheduling.

What's more, the Army's Life Cycle Management Commands (LCMCs – mentioned back in the 'OIB' chapter) began to hold monthly meetings to discuss anticipated changes in future materiel requirements and resource constraints. These management reviews also helped mitigate potential supply chain problems.

But other problems in supply chain operations remained to be solved. For example, insufficient access to data sometimes led to inaccurate and unsynchronized lists of parts for engineering, procurement, and repair. And, changes that were made to manufacturing processes in response to the evolution of tactical operations overseas and equipment upgrades were not always captured in these lists (known as bills of materiel). This produced bottlenecks and delays. Plus, systematic errors prevented the all-important Army Enterprise Systems Integration Program (or 'AESIP' – another cornerstone of its ERP programs) database from displaying orders and information on the bills of materiel. This too resulted in production delays and inventory shortages. LMP, especially its second version, addressed these and other problems, with each LMP upgrade providing enhanced logistical capabilities and a clearer picture of the entire supply chain pipeline.

The Army also began transitioning from applying rather minimal supplier performance standards and accepting the lowest bids toward more stringent and strategic sourcing and resource management. By establishing longer-term relationships with industry partners to facilitate open dialogue and synergy, the Army improved supplier performance. Further, technical data were continually reviewed, updated, and verified, allowing the Army to reduce inventory levels and divest itself of unneeded property. Reduced inventory, greater production efficiencies resulting from more accurate bills of materiel, purchases of newer manufacturing machinery, and other changes enabled the Army's OIB to operate more economically. As the Army divests itself of unneeded property, energy and water costs decline. Ultimately, strategic sourcing promises to not only lower the costs of materiel and equipment but also to improve warfighter performance.

Army leaders in the Organic Industrial Base gained a more comprehensive understanding of the entire business process through use of ERP and LMP. Earlier methods of managing the Army's supply requirements often involved minimal coordination between business departments. But their broader understanding enabled leaders to make more informed decisions and to better anticipate their potential effects.

LMP is not only providing major logistical benefits to the Army, it is doing so at a reasonable cost. In fact, the total projected financial benefit of LMP – through the year 2026 – is estimated at over $2 billion.

ERP and LMP are proving to be sound investments for the U.S. Army. These programs enable the Army to supply and sustain its forces with materiel and equipment that is tailorable, scalable, and rapidly deployable to achieve the capability to prevail over the enemy's forces anywhere in the world. In short, they enable materiel readiness to defend and promote the nation's interests. ERP has also proven to be a smart investment for U.S. businesses.

Takeaways:

* The rapid delivery of material and supplies, whether in the military or the business world, is more critical than ever
* Enterprise Resource Planning, an integrated logistics information technology system, is a must for efficient and effective supply chain operations
* If ERP is done right, there is a significant return on investment
* That said, there's still plenty of work to be done to better integrate our ERPs to gain the ROI we need

CHAPTER 9

THE CYBER THREAT AND THE SUPPLY CHAIN
(Yes, It's Vulnerable)

In April 2015, security engineers at the Office of Personnel Management (OPM), which is the human resources agency for the federal government, discovered some particularly unnerving malware in the agency's digital systems. It was intended to give hackers access to the department's servers. OPM was fending off 10 million attempted digital infiltrations a month at the time; a year earlier, an attack had stolen blueprints for its digital network's architecture. With the current breach, the hackers had obtained access to every bit of the agency's digital terrain. And not only had the malware been on the network for nearly a year, the assault had been carried out by a hacker group that was believed to have launched some of the most damaging cyberattacks in recent years. They included a penetration of the health insurer Anthem that led to the pilfering of the personal data of close to 80 million Americans. There was persuasive evidence that these hackers were tied to China, with its reportedly 100,000-strong cyber-espionage force. Yet, no one knew with certainty the hackers' intentions.[10]

Four months later, in August 2015, hackers gained access to the unclassified email network of the Joint Chiefs of Staff (JCS), the nation's highest-ranking military command. The opening of one malicious email unleashed the turmoil that followed. The hackers stole the passwords and electronic signatures of the chairman of the JCS and hundreds of other top military officers to sign on to the network. The only way to stop the assault was to shut down the system, leaving the JCS's several thousand employees without email for nearly two weeks while hardware and software were replaced. These hackers, which U.S. officials said were Russians (others disagreed), apparently sought to simply wreak damage and havoc.[11]

The Department of Defense, which is equipped with highly sophisticated, state-of-the-art cyber defense technology, suffers over 10 million breach attempts every day *(mainly the sorts of scans and phishing that afflict any large organization, hence the mind-boggling volume)*. U.S. government databases are choice targets for our adversaries.[12]

---

10 Brendan I. Koerner, "Inside the Cyberattack That Shocked the US Government," Wired, October 23, 2016.

11 "Russian Hackers Hit Pentagon Email System in 2015: CBS," Reuters, December 15, 2016; Bradley Barth, "Report: Russian Hackers Breached Joint Chiefs' Email System in 2015," SC Media, December 20, 2016.

12 This chapter is based mainly on Larry Wyche and Dawn Dunkerley Goss, "Attacking the Cyber Challenge"; Larry Wyche and Greg Pieratt, "Securing the Army's Weapon Systems and Supply Chain against Cyber Attack," Institute of Land Warfare, Association of the U.S. Army, November 2017; and Larry Wyche and Dawn Dunkerley Goss, "Attacking Cyber: Increasing Resilience and Protecting Mission Essential Capabilities in Cyberspace," The Cyber Defense Review, Summer-Fall 2016.

America's potential adversaries in the cyber world generally fall into three categories: states such as Russia, China, North Korea, and Iran; non-state actors including ISIS and Al-Qaeda; and criminals. The states often work with non-state actors and possess advanced cyber capabilities and a motive to steal information to gain military or economic advantage. Recently, partly in response to President Donald Trump's withdrawal from the 2015 U.S. nuclear agreement with Iran and trade disputes with China, Iran and China revived their hacking of U.S. companies and government agencies after an earlier cooling. Dozens of corporations were hit (though it was unclear how many of the attacks were successful). China sought to steal trade and military secrets from U.S. military contractors and technology companies. Boeing, General Electric Aviation, and T-Mobile were among the targets of China's efforts at industrial espionage. Iran, in addition to attacking Internet service providers, telecommunications companies, and other corporations, struck over a half dozen government agencies in one month. "Cyber is one of the ways adversaries can attack us and retaliate in effective and nasty ways that are well below the threshold of an armed attack or laws of war," Joel Brenner, a former U.S. counterintelligence official, commented to the *New York Times*. "If you tell the Iranians you're going to walk out on the agreement and do everything you can to undermine their government, you can't be surprised if they attack our government networks."[13]

ISIS and Al-Qaeda, who sometimes work with states, also have advanced cyber capabilities and a desire to steal information. ISIS has hacked websites and social media accounts and even reportedly

13 New York Times, February 18, 2019.

has a hacking wing. Criminal elements hack systems mainly to obtain access to financial data and other information for monetary gain.

Members of all three groups of adversaries' scan systems to plan penetrations by employing phishing, Trojans, and other techniques. They execute their attacks through software that finds unpatched (i.e. not yet fixed to provide security) cyber terrain through which they can infiltrate, use traveling worms that attach themselves to emails, and engage in other schemes. They are capable of conducting highly sophisticated, coordinated series of attacks on email systems and servers to steal information. All three categories of actors have the ability to severely disrupt and destroy digital systems.

Through cyber warfare, America's foes are capable of playing havoc with our military operations by targeting our command and control, weapon systems, logistical systems (including our ERP systems – and SALE), the industrial base that manufactures and repairs our weapons, and the supply chain that sustains them. As Greg Pieratt and I wrote in 2017, "The Army's weapon systems and the supply chain that supports them are now more vulnerable than ever."[14] We weren't being alarmist.

Compromises to our ERP systems and the planting of counterfeit or sabotaged components and microchips into our supply inventory are two of the biggest dangers. Most breaches of ERP systems originate in the supply chain. The Army has thousands of top-tier suppliers and must permit them access to its systems in order to obtain real-time visibility of assets. This creates vulnerabilities, as each of these suppliers has at least hundreds of other

14 Wyche and Pieratt, "Securing."

suppliers supporting them. Subcontractors, who often lack the latest security measures, are the softest targets. And once adversaries manage to get inside ERP systems, they can change schedules, alter parts lists, and engage in an unlimited number of other disruptive acts.

Hackings, including malware implants, into Army systems have mushroomed over the past decade. The attacks have grown increasingly innovative with use of new, advanced technologies, while use of affordable, widely available technologies has also grown. The vulnerability of U.S. cyber assets is increasing exponentially. And it would not be an exaggeration to say that the next war might well be decided in cyber space.

Consider the following scenario: An aggressor launches an invasion of a nation allied with the United States, and U.S. troops are deployed to the country. Suddenly, peculiar things start to happen. Ground-to-ground missiles malfunction, the aggressor takes control of U.S. satellites, anti-aircraft missiles consistently fail to hit their targets, and U.S. artillery strike friendly forces. When the arsenals, depots, and ammunition plants in the Army's Organic Industrial Base kick into overdrive to support the U.S. military campaign, there are more odd developments: the wrong parts are ordered, errors on shipping manifests send items pell-mell in the wrong directions, and the water and power systems of Army installations go haywire.

It is subsequently determined that the enemy may have used one of the latest cyber war tactics, a "zero-day attack" that exploits a newly discovered software vulnerability that has no fix yet or takes place before the vulnerability is known by the software's users. It turns out attackers had exploited unknown flaws in our weapon and logistics systems.

This scenario is not all that far-fetched, except perhaps in the extreme. A cyberattack on the Army's logistics systems could be absolutely calamitous.

The U.S. Transportation Command (USTRANSCOM) is the unified combatant command responsible for transporting U.S. troops and distributing military equipment worldwide. From 2008 to 2013, on numerous occasions, hackers launched zero-day and phishing attacks to penetrate the information systems used by contractors working for USTRANSCOM. Over the course of one year, 2012–2013, around 50 such attacks took place. And at least 20 were successful.

Hackers have also infiltrated important U.S. weapon systems, including the UH-60 Black Hawk helicopter and the Patriot missile system. Hackers installed remote-access kits and downloaded blueprints and other proprietary information. They also inserted a "backdoor," or secret portal, that allowed them to repeatedly return to gather system updates until they were finally detected.

How do they do it? One way is through using altered firmware, which is software built by a vendor that controls the key functions of weapon systems. To lower development costs, firmware is often created from off-the-shelf or open-source software, which makes exploitation fairly easy. And once they've penetrated a system, attackers can insert passcodes that will grant them access later. Or, they might pretend to be a legitimate member of a communication network, executing a "man-in-the-middle" attack, and intercept and alter commands that way.

In one frightening case, attackers exploited firmware in hand-held scanners used by shipping, warehousing, and delivery services. They gained access to technical details about ships, shipping manifests, and other corporate information. Later, they transferred control of the entire distribution network to their servers. Fortunately, a security company working for the U.S. Department of Homeland Security discovered the infiltration.

Perhaps even more unsettling, the electronic components in missiles, smart munitions (including bombs), helicopters, tanks, and other combat vehicles and weapons are often built using commercial off-the-shelf technology, including computer chips. And adversaries can plant malware into the chips that arrest or change their function.

The U.S. Army Materiel Command (mentioned first in the chapter on the OIB) employs hundreds of systems and applications, thousands of servers, and an enormous amount of other network infrastructure. Without an effective cyber defense, the potential points of cyberattack against the command would be almost endless.

Mitigating the Threat

From 2015-2017, U.S. Army Materiel Command led, with the help of Dr. Dawn Dunkerley and a great staff, the development and execution of the AMC's cyber security strategy. AMC and the U.S. Army Cyber Command (which operates and defends the Army's information network) worked overtime to beef up our cyber defenses. We did everything we could to protect U.S. weapons and logistical systems, network infrastructure, supply chains, and the industrial base from cyberattacks. And after investing considerable time and resources, and despite underfunding, we made significant progress. AMC employed an aggressive, three-step approach to enhance our defensive cyber capabilities, one it continues to use and refine today.

The first step, "seeing yourself," entails creating a picture of your organization—its missions, competencies, goals, priorities, and actions needed to attain them—and how it carries out its operations in cyberspace. This step also involves mapping critical cyber terrain by identifying what information systems and applications are needed to execute the command's mission, who uses these systems and applications, and where they're located. AMC's current cyber terrain map depicts users and decision-makers, their devices and IP addresses, the databases and websites they need, network infrastructure, and the physical locations from which information is accessed.

The second step in AMC's process is "understanding risk and recognizing gaps." This involves knowing which networks, data, and systems architecture absolutely must be defended to prevent the disruption of operations. It also entails assessing the vulnerabilities in the systems and the applications that attackers might exploit. Comprehending data flow across devices used by suppliers, their data storage and retrieval applications, and the hardware and infrastructure used is key to identifying weak points. This step also involves recognizing where the vulnerabilities are located and assessing the likelihood of attacks and their potential severity. In addition, it entails identifying the potential attackers—state, non-state, criminal, or even insiders—and analyzing their capabilities and intentions. Finally, it includes understanding the difference between the level of cyber protection needed and the reality: the gaps. Are our actions sufficient to attain that protection and minimize our vulnerabilities?

The third step is "implementing mitigation strategies and managing residual risk." This involves determining the actions, resources, technology, and expertise needed to close the gaps. It entails sharing cyber threat intelligence among personnel, incorporating this intelligence into training and reinforcing it in memos and meetings, and directing cyber security cells to monitor operational risk and track malware infiltrations. It also includes conducting operations using paper at times instead of a digital system, integrating cyber security personnel into software development groups, certifying suppliers, implementing strict protocols to prevent hidden and unwanted access to the supply chain, and providing real-time status reports on threats and vulnerability. In addition, outside experts should be tapped to increase understanding of threats and vulnerability, and networks should be modernized. While there will always be security risks despite these mitigation strategies, they must be minimized and managed effectively.

The Army has developed other countermeasures to cyberattacks in order to protect its supply chain as well. While deployed fairly recently, they have shown great promise. One is isolating the critical functions of weapon system components and developing fail-safe methods to make sure they cannot be disrupted. Another is applying rigorous enforcement standards for inspecting electrical components, integrated circuitry, and circuit boards supplied by vendors to ensure that they contain no malicious code. Still another is buying computer chips only from trusted semiconductor plants with tough quality and inspection standards, while making sure that suppliers do not get their chips from cheaper, third-party factories. The Army's countermeasures also include using tamper-resistant packaging to prevent replacement of components with counterfeit ones while they are in transit, making "blind buys" from low-risk suppliers who are not aware of the use of the components they supply, and utilizing "separation kernels" to guarantee that software applications cannot affect one another, thereby preventing the spread of malware. Finally, the Army is using tighter language in contracts to provide for stricter accountability and harsher penalties for suppliers who take shortcuts and employing "red teams" who utilize the most advanced cyber methods to ferret out vulnerabilities.

Every time those involved in America's supply chain operations enter cyberspace, they must recognize that they are entering contested terrain. And anticipating cyber threats to our systems and networks should be standard procedure. The same is true in the corporate world: you can never be too vigilant about cyberattacks and the need to safeguard your systems.

While protecting America's weapons systems, supply chain, and industrial base from cyberattacks will require continual work and refinement in the years ahead, we cannot let down our guard. We have no other choice: our nation's security is at stake.

Takeaways:

* The cyber threat to our logistics operations and global supply chains is real and growing
* Planning aggressive countermeasures can mitigate – but not eliminate – this threat
* What's your plan against cyberattacks?

CHAPTER 10:

CONTRACTING & MONEY

(They're Weapon Systems)

In 1985, I was a young captain, and my wife, Denise, was working as an Army civilian contracting officer while we were raising three kids. Over the next 25 years, Denise excelled at contracting, which is a very complex and demanding career. She served at numerous organizations, including the Tank-Automotive and Armaments Command and the Defense Contract Management Agency. She managed contracts worth millions of dollars.

Like many husbands, I should have listened more to my wife about a lot of things. Although I always fully supported her career, I should have paid more attention to her dinner-table stories about contracting and her experiences with contract negotiation and management. My wife shared her challenges, her successes and how much she enjoyed her work. Too often, I'd pretend to listen, but my mind was on my work for the next day, or the next week. If the Minnesota Vikings were on television, I didn't even pretend to listen.

Of course, I wasn't fooling her. She'd tell me, *"Honey, you're not listening to me,"* and it was true.

Defense contracting is hard to understand. It has its own vocabulary and can take years to master. Part of me knew how important contracting was to military commands, but I'd managed to avoid having too much to do with it and hadn't even learned the basics. I wasn't "smart" on it.

Big mistake. Especially since I had an expert right in my own house!

Years later, during my deployment to Afghanistan, when I led the Joint Logistics Command, which included overseeing multimillion-dollar contracts, I went through a steep and at times painful learning curve on contracting. *"I should have listened more to my wife,"* I often muttered to myself.

In U.S. counterinsurgency operations, money is a weapon. Money gets the military the things it needs to function in austere places like Afghanistan. We provided money for transporting materiel, digging wells, building schools, and hundreds of other things there. Money also generates economic activity, spurs employment, and can reward and reinforce ethical business practices by contractors. And if used effectively, it can dissuade potential allies from working with violent extremist organizations who often rely on corruption and crime to fund terrorist activities.

U.S. military forces use money to pay for products or services provided by private-sector contractors. Some of these contractors are small and local, while others are large and operate on a regional or even global scale (think Raytheon or Boeing). Given the importance of these contracts, the U.S. military's contracting experts are essential to modern warfare. Actually, contracting has always been important to U.S. warfighting. From the American Revolution (when contractors provided services, clothing, and weapons) through the American Civil War (when the public sector provided construction, transportation, and other services) on up to Vietnam and Desert Storm (when contractors substantially supplemented the Organic Industrial Base), contracting has always been a part of how we fight.[15] In fact, the more I learned about it, the stranger it seemed that we don't usually train senior military leaders in even the basics of contracting before they take command.

I've already mentioned one reason we don't—because it's super complicated. Another is that soldiers are generally more comfortable with things like rifles, automatic weapons, artillery, and tanks than they are with contracting and money. And military contracting (often with good reason) is one of those functions that comes with tons of oversight. Even junior military officers and NCOs can find themselves responsible for contracts worth millions of dollars, and there is little tolerance for error in the execution of these con-

---

15 "Contingency Contracting Throughout U.S. History," https://www.acq.osd.mil/dpap/pacc/cc/history.html.

tracts. The Inspector General of the Department of Defense, organizations like SIGAR (which oversees reconstruction projects in Afghanistan), and even the U.S. Congress and the media can be ruthless in enforcing (some might call it "second-guessing") rigorous adherence to contracting regulations and decisions made under the stress of combat operations. I imagine that if someone asked an average Army officer or NCO whether they'd rather be on a combat patrol in Afghanistan or be responsible for contracts on a multimillion-dollar construction project, they'd take the combat patrol, hands down.

In my case, after about two months in Afghanistan, we were doing pretty well in terms of our logistics operations. However, we had *major* problems working with the legion of Afghan and Pakistani trucking companies we hired and with Pakistani authorities, who closed the two major routes into Afghanistan and charged us ridiculous tariffs. Most aggravating, a lot of our materiel and supplies were being stolen. *Pilfered* is the more diplomatic term normally used in circumstances like these. Whatever anyone else called it, we were getting robbed. Every. Single. Day.

Our task force would easily have 300 to 500 Afghan and Pakistani jingle trucks on the road carrying food, water, fuel, and repair parts at any given time. *(I mentioned these trucks in an earlier chapter.)*

Jingle trucks get their name from the colorful, elaborate floral patterns and calligraphy the drivers and operators use to decorate their vehicles. It came as a surprise to me, but we did not have one American military truck company in Afghanistan. There were two reasons for that, the first being that there was a cap on how many soldiers could be in the country at one time, and we were better served with combat soldiers. The second was simply safety and a desire to keep U.S. soldiers out of harm's way. Therefore, we relied on Afghan and Pakistani trucking companies and operators.

With the huge ground-distribution problem we had in Afghanistan, the bulk of our supplies traveled to Afghanistan through a Pakistan seaport (Afghanistan has no ports since it's a landlocked country). Supplies were then loaded onto Pakistani jingle trucks. These trucks would travel hundreds of miles through desert and mountains to our operating bases in Afghanistan. In the case of those carrying fuel, the jingle trucks would load their contents into giant bags at a fuel supply points. These bags could hold anywhere from 10,000 to 50,000 gallons of fuel. The fuel would then either be stored or transferred to an Afghan jingle truck and delivered to units operating in forward locations, some in very remote places that required the drivers to negotiate even harsher terrain.

On top of the sheer logistical difficulties, our supplies were highly vulnerable to pilferage. To say that theft was widespread would be an understatement. Besides outright stealing of supplies, we had to contend with an extensive informal system of bribery, whereby bribes were offered to Afghan drivers in return for supplies (a tempting proposition for many drivers); other drivers felt compelled to turn over supplies to thieves just to stay alive.

Driving a jingle truck was, in fact, one of the most dangerous jobs on the planet at the time. Many Afghan drivers traveling through violent tribal territories were killed. As a result of theft, bribery, and violence directed at the drivers, at times only 70 percent of the supplies made it to our forward operating bases. To put it mildly, this was a major problem.

As the commander, I had two worries. I was sure I'd either fail to get something to a unit under fire, or that my boss or I would be hauled in front of a congressional committee back in the beltway for a nasty grilling about our lapses.

The owners of the trucking companies were often wealthy individuals. Some were honest business people (or aspired to be) doing their best under impossible circumstances. But many others were corrupt. Frankly, I did not know who I could trust, and I always wanted a lawyer right beside me when dealing with the contractors. I consistently made it clear to the trucking companies that we did not take shortcuts, that we operated by the letter of the law, and that if they could not adhere to those standards, they were not doing business in the right place. My team conveyed the same message at every opportunity because we wanted to send a clear statement of our values and how we operated as an Army.

Using money as a weapon, we threatened the owners of the trucking companies with losing contracts if they didn't clean up their operations. With trucking in support of U.S. military operations such a lucrative venture, the owners did not want to lose all that money.

We also conducted a detailed analysis of how each contract company performed. We then presented the overall results to all the owners and then shared with each owner (one-on-one) how their company was performing. We reinforced companies that were doing well with more work and money; companies that were not doing well were warned that they needed to get their operations in order. Several were suspended or terminated. I can recall one of our meetings being really intense. Initially, some contractors thought we were bluffing when we threatened to terminate their contracts, until we began to show them their performance stats. Then the conversation got very serious, and they quickly realized that they were on the verge of not having a job. In fact, there was one contractor who we suspended and who then attempted to bribe someone on our team. He quickly found himself not doing business with the Army.

Since we were facing a systemic problem, we never achieved a 100 percent delivery rate—it simply wasn't possible. There was no way we'd ever eliminate the network of bribes, illicit payments, and thievery that plagued our ground transport mission. Still, we were able to increase the delivery rate to the low-to-mid 90 percent level. That, we thought, was a considerable accomplishment. We had to balance the need to adhere to U.S. standards of government contracting and our responsibility as public servants – with the painful and exasperating realization that corruption was a fact of life in Afghanistan. This was quite difficult for me and my team.

But I came to know and to have tremendous respect for many of the Afghan and Pakistani trucking company leaders I negotiated with. They operated in an unforgiving world. They could not often appeal to the rule of law or impartial courts or judges. Aside from contending with constant offers of bribes and outright theft of supplies, they had to make off-the-record payments to customs inspectors and government regulators and administrators. These payments were simply part of daily business; nothing would get done without them. The trucking companies were squeezed all around. But as the senior logistics commander, my team had to deliver to our soldiers – and adhere to the law. At the end of the day, we had to understand the country that we were operating in and recognize that we were not going to change the business culture overnight, all while not compromising our values or duties as Army leaders and soldiers.

Other Lessons on Contracting

Military contracting is big business. Real big. To give you an idea of its magnitude, the U.S. Army Contracting Command awarded over $50 billion in contracts in 2016. The top U.S. defense contractors each do billions of dollars of weapons sales each year.

I was naive about all that in my early years as an Army officer, just as I was naive about the Army's Organic Industrial Base and all of its government-owned equipment facilities. I never had any real idea where the supplies and materiel my units needed came from. They just seemed to show up.

After I had been selected for brigadier general in 2008, I was assigned to the Joint Munitions and Lethality Life Cycle Management Command, which was split between the Picatinny Arsenal in New Jersey and the Rock Island Arsenal in Illinois. The command's mission is to "develop, acquire, field, and sustain value-added ammunition for joint warfighters through the integration of effective and timely acquisition, logistics, and cutting-edge technology." That's a mouthful, but sufficed to say that the command is essential to providing munitions to U.S. warfighters. Both the Picatinny and Rock Island Arsenals are among those places that most people have never heard of, but which our military could not do without. They are critical to overseeing the Army's organic ammunition facilities, and they produce and store millions of tons of ammunition that supply our armed forces daily.

As the commanding general—and this is a lesson in the importance of always reading the fine print when you take command — I was also the "head of contracting activities" (HCA). In other words, I was the "official who has overall responsibility for managing a contracting activity." A "contracting activity" is an element of an agency that has broad authority over procurement and acquisition – and oversight of multimillion-dollar contracts.

Lucky me.

Being an HCA is a demanding undertaking, especially for someone who had until this point in my career not fully appreciated the value of contracting and its indispensability to the Army.

Fortunately, I had an exceptional and seasoned attorney, Kathi Szymanski, who had worked in contracting for years. "Sir, I have not had a commander go to jail yet, and I don't plan on you being the first," she assured me. What a relief that was. Kathi was very good at her job, and she made sure I was always prepared; there was never a question of me or the command acting in a way that was inconsistent with the intent of the regulations and governing authorities. Something as simple as seeing one contractor and not another prior to a solicitation could spell trouble because a person could draw the inference that you were favoring one contractor over another. These were among the many things that Kathi really stayed on top of.

If you are a military logistician, pay close attention, because you may be responsible for contracting duties like these someday:

- Ensuring that all contract actions comply with the law and acquisition regulations
- Ensuring that only properly warranted contract officers execute contracting actions
- Encouraging the development and application of innovative contracting methods and other acquisition reforms
- Approving procurement decisions, and when appropriate, authorizing waivers or exceptions that the law or regulations allow
- Providing oversight and promoting standardized contracting policies and procedures throughout the contracting offices and activities within the organization

And, if you're lucky enough to be married to a Department of Defense contracting officer like I was, listen to her. It will spare you many headaches down the road.

At the end of the day, I survived my tour as an Army contracting official, just as I had survived my tour in Afghanistan. But I was left with some bumps and bruises, and I still had lots to learn about military contracting.

Types of Contracts and Organizations

A military contracting official has to learn about the many different types of contracts. And not only that, they have to determine in any given situation which contract is more advantageous to the government as opposed to being advantageous to the contractor. Learning these contract types and the choices they presented was a major task for me – contracting professionals can spend an entire career mastering this skill. I had to accept the fact that I would never be a contracting expert, but I figured that if I learned the basics and knew the right questions to ask, I would be all right.

For example, I discovered that just knowing the basic difference between a Firm-Fixed Price contract, in which the contractor assumes the risks inherent in the contract, and a Cost-Plus-Incentive contract, in which the government assumes the risks while benefiting if the actual cost of the product is lower than the expected cost, was extremely helpful. I don't want to oversimplify contracting, because it's quite complex and there are numerous types of contracts. But the point is that you have to roll up your sleeves, get your hands dirty, and really start learning.

It's also important that you take the time to become familiar with the various types of contracting organizations and their responsibilities. Within the U.S. Army Materiel Command, for example, the Army Contracting Command (ACC) is a subordinate unit responsible for delivering Army readiness and supporting modernization through smart contracting. Other key contracting organizations can be found within the U.S. Army Corps of Engineers, the U.S. Army Medical Command, and the Army National Guard and Reserve.

AMC, by way of the ACC, was the Army's workhorse when it came to contracting. It was easily responsible for 75 percent of the Army's contracting. On average, at AMC, we completed over $50 billion in contract awards yearly, with $8 billion of that going to small businesses – as mentioned earlier. Eight billion dollars is not chump change, and the small business program is fixed in statute. It was established under the Small Business Act of 1953, with the intent to ensure that a fair portion of the government's total purchases through both prime and subcontracts were placed with small businesses, including disadvantaged ones. Small Business Categories include (and you should be familiar with these):

A. Small businesses overall
B. Small disadvantaged businesses
C. Women-owned small businesses
D. HUBZone small businesses
E. Service-disabled, veteran-owned small businesses

Within AMC, we had a small business office that was responsible for implementing the small business program. And if AMC did not meet its small business goals, the Army did not meet its goals. Therefore, this heightened the pressure to produce.

Acquisition

At the end of the day, military contracting, like logistics, is about getting the right equipment into the hands of our soldiers when they need it. Sounds pretty simple. But it's far from simple, especially when you are dealing with major weapons systems, such as tanks, aircraft, and vehicle radios, to mention just a few. It's essential that the contract team is in sync with the acquisition people at every step of the acquisition process—from analysis to deployment to support—to guarantee the timely fulfillment of the contracting requirements. As a young Army officer, I did not take the time to learn the relationship between contracting and acquisition *(this is becoming quite a recurring theme of the book, I realize)*. Frankly, I felt it was not my concern, so why waste my time trying to learn something that I would not be doing? But as I grew to recognize and appreciate the significance of contracting and its relationship to acquisition, I realized how naive I'd been. I also found that understanding the various phases of what's known as the "Defense Acquisition Life Cycle" was a great way to start my learning process. All require contracting support and thus a lot of attention.

Putting together the right contracting and acquisition teams requires literally thousands of hours of hard work. But the results can be very rewarding. In 2017, the contracting team headed by

Rebecca (Becky) Wierick at Redstone Arsenal in Alabama signed a $3.8 billion, five-year contract with Sikorsky to purchase 257 Black Hawk utility helicopters for the Army and foreign military sales. The arsenal's contracting office personnel did exceptional work negotiating a contract that saved the Army $822 million (by reducing the cost by that amount from Sikorsky's bid) while at the same creating a win-win situation for all parties, especially by providing the Army and foreign military partners with the right capabilities. Those of us involved in Army contracting have not always been that effective at negotiating a favorable result for the Army. This was a major success for the Army's acquisition and contracting communities.[16]

On the other hand, contracting and acquisition teams can do all the right things during the acquisition and contracting processes, but still face congressional and public protest of the contracts they negotiated. In its 2015 report to Congress, the Government Accounting Office noted that the number of such protests had increased by 2–3 percent per year since 2011. I learned that there are a number of reasons for them, ranging from a shrinking defense budget and fiscal pressures to truly believing that a mistake or misjudgment was made in negotiating the contract.

---

16 Multiyear production contract for Black Hawk helicopters saves Army $800 million, Mr. Paul Stevenson (PEO Aviation); available at: https://www.army.mil/ article/191541/multiyear_production_contract_for_black_hawk_helicopters_ saves_army_800_million

The Federal Budget and Appropriations

Even with the best contracting and acquisition teams, but, of course, you still need money to award contracts. So, having at least a basic familiarity with the federal budget and the appropriations process is important if you're involved with government contracting. I was probably a major in the Army before I was forced to learn about budgets, appropriations, and fiscal years, and why they mattered. It turned out they mattered a lot.

You have heard hundreds of times the saying "follow the money." Well, that's true with contracting as well. The federal government funds innumerable programs and activities ranging from social programs to scientific research to military operations, and roughly two-thirds of federal spending is "mandatory spending"— to include, Social Security, Medicaid, and Medicare. Mandatory spending is enacted by law and does not depend upon appropriations. The other category of federal spending is "discretionary" a significant portion of which consists of defense spending. Discretionary programs have limits on funding that can be provided within a fiscal year.

The federal funding process begins with the submission of the president's annual budget request to Congress. Traditionally, this is done on the first Monday in February. Once the president's budget request is submitted, Congress drafts a budget resolution. The budget resolution establishes a total level of discretionary funding for the upcoming fiscal year. The funding process then moves to the appropriations committees in each chamber of Congress. These committees are responsible for funding discretionary programs. Twelve separate appropriation bills are generated by these subcommittees. Of greatest interest to the Army, the Department of Defense's allocations are first developed by the Subcommittees on Defense of the House and Senate Appropriations Committees. These are often referred to as the 'HAC-D' and 'SAC-D'.

Public hearings are often held as part of this process and involve senior uniformed and civilian defense leaders. In fact, the Secretary of Defense, Chairman of the Joint Chiefs, Service Secretariess and Service Chiefs will usually testify annually. The culmination of this effort is typically a bill that'll be voted on by the full appropriations committee.

The bills then go before the full House and Senate for a approval. Usually, the next step is for the House and Senate to engage in a joint conference to negotiate over any differences in their respective bills. The goal of all this is for a defense appropriations bill to be passed and sent to the President by the end of September, in time for a new fiscal year. Unfortunately, in recent years, this hasn't occurred. To keep the government from shutting down, Congress enacts something called a continuing resolution (CRs). These are short-term bills that keep funding levels the same as the prior year. One of the many problems with CRs is that the Defense Department usually can't start new programs. This makes predictable, consistent funding for things like research, development, and acquisition, very difficult to plan.[17]

17 The material for this Chapter is derived from a U.S. Army information paper titled "The Federal Budget and Appropriations Process." There are many excellent sources that depict how the budget process works, to include "The Congressional Appropriations Process: an Introduction" by the Congressional Research Service; Nov, 2016.

Obtaining funding for defense programs, including to pay for contracts, is a long and arduous process. But if you work in the field of defense contracting, you have to know this process from end to end, just as you need to know about types of contracts, the government bodies that handle defense contracts, the acquisition process, and all the other nitty-gritty of the contracting process. Take your time to learn it. It will pay off!

Takeaways:

* It's never too early to learn the ins and outs of contracting and acquisition
* Understand DoD and Army contracting organizations and what they can do for you
* View contracting as a capability
* Take the time to learn (a little) about the federal budget and appropriations process

CHAPTER 11:

THOUGHTS ON
LOGISTICS LEADERSHIP

It's hard to think of a topic that has been written about, talked about, thought about, argued about, and analyzed more than leadership. All around the globe, there are thousands of college courses and advanced degrees offered on *leadership*. Countless books, media stories, academic articles, and websites are produced—with more arriving every minute—about leadership: *What is it? What it isn't? Who has it? Who doesn't? How do you learn it? How do you teach it? How do you recognize it? How can you be a good leader? — or at least, How can you avoid being a terrible one?* The list goes on and on.

Leadership is often spoken about as if it's some kind of magic potion or fairy dust. Sprinkle enough of it on any organization, and you'll get results. You'll increase profits, improve morale, win a battle, or a war. With the mystical qualities often attributed to leadership, everything is possible, and conversely, without it, nothing is possible. If we could just bottle this leadership stuff up and serve it in the mess hall or office cafeteria, many of our most vexing challenges would be resolved. We'd arrive at the office each day to fulfilled, self-motivated team members, all creatively and diligently working toward the right goal in an environment where fairness, dignity, and mutual respect reign supreme.

Well, maybe.

I'd bet some of you have already read a great deal on leadership over the course of your life. If you're in business and went to a business school, you no doubt studied it. If you're in the military, you've received leadership instruction since the day you first put on the uniform. In fact, few organizations devote as much time, commitment, and effort to understanding and honing leadership as our armed forces do. In fact, I've benefited tremendously from the leadership training the Army provided me.

If the opening paragraph of this chapter sounded a bit dismissive or cynical to your ears, my tone only reflects the dizzying variety and sheer volume of leadership material out there, along with the superficial and contradictory nature of much of it. It's all too easy to find books written by great leaders and great students of leadership that appear to say one thing, only to say nearly the exact opposite thing a few pages later. How many times have you read leadership tips like "Good leaders don't micromanage their employees," only to read a few pages later something like *"Good leaders pay attention to the smallest details."*

Or:

"Good leaders stay focused on the big picture" vs. *"Good leaders know what every part of their organization does"*

"*Good leaders gather input from a wide variety of people before making decisions*" vs. "*Good leaders avoid paralysis by analysis and make decisions promptly*"

"*Good leaders are kind, compassionate and respectful*" vs. "*Good leaders are tough as nails and speak the plain, blunt truth even if it hurts*"

"*Good leaders are patient*" vs. "*Good leaders move fast*"

"*Good leaders are confident*" vs. "*Good leaders are humble*"

"*Good leaders are visible*" vs. "*Good leaders know when to stay in the background*"

"*Good leaders focus on things that can be measured*" vs. "*Good leaders don't get bogged down in numbers and statistics*"

For almost every trait or characteristic of great leadership, we can find examples where doing the exact opposite seemed to work just as well. After reading a lot about leadership, you might feel as if you'd gotten a case of whiplash from all of the contradictory advice.

Despite all of this, there are few more vital subjects to explore. Over the years, I've witnessed firsthand the difference that the right leadership can make for an organization. I've had the privilege of serving under and learning from some of the most talented leaders in the armed forces and private industry. I've also learned a great deal (maybe even more) from the examples of poor leadership I've encountered. Fortunately, there haven't been many of those (I might be just plain lucky in that regard), but a number of bad-leadership lessons have stuck with me—sometimes painfully.

So, at the risk of committing some of the sins of the leadership advice mentioned above, I want to offer a few lessons that have served me well. Feel free to take 'em or leave 'em, or compare 'em to what's worked for you and what you've seen work for others.

You've Got to Want to Be in Charge

All too often, many of us assume, without a lot of reflection, that becoming a supervisor, manager, or higher-level leader is just the logical next step in whatever career we're pursuing. In the military, such stepwise progression is largely the norm, and taking on greater leadership responsibilities is the consequence of accepting a promotion. The higher you go in the service, the broader, more substantial, and more challenging your leadership duties are certain to become.

However, in my experience, few of us really stop and consider whether we want to be leaders. Do you honestly want to be put in charge? By that I don't mean to ask if you want the increased pay, the greater prestige, the bigger office, or that nice reserved parking space for your new car. *(After all, who wouldn't want that?)*

What I mean is, do you want to be held accountable for the work, actions, and performance of other people? Do you want to provide direction that helps people work toward a common goal? Do you want to set objectives, timetables, and milestones, while making and enforcing plans that are carried out by others? Do you want to help others work together, build a cohesive team, and resolve the personal conflicts (often intense, sometimes bitter, and more than occasionally irrational and exasperating) that arise in every organization? Do you have the fortitude to give orders, see that they are executed, and counsel or discipline people who don't meet the standard? Do you want to spend the majority of your workday not as an expert in a particular subject but rather as the manager and leader of other subject-matter experts? Finally, do you genuinely like people? *(Okay, you don't have to like every single one. But, in general, misanthropes don't make good leaders.)*

Rather than simply accepting a leadership position because you're on career autopilot and it's the next step to getting a promotion or a raise, it's important to ask yourself questions like these, and even more vital that you answer them honestly. You're the only one who truly knows the answers. If your candid self-assessment yields a lot of no's, it might be worth taking another look at your career choice and the path ahead of you. There are few things worse than embarking on a profession that's going to make you *(and the people around you)* unhappy. Not everyone wants to be in charge, and not everyone should seek to be in charge. And there's nothing wrong with that. There are millions of exceptionally talented people in every walk of life who go to work each day and make invaluable contributions to their organizations without being leaders. They design new products, develop new services, find new cures for diseases, write great advertising campaigns, and make brilliant arguments in courts of law. Just because you have a great skill or are the smartest person in the conference room doesn't mean you'll make a great supervisor, manager, or higher leader. This is a fact of life that many would-be leaders do not want to face.

Ask yourself:

• Is the most brilliant and skilled surgeon always the best choice to become CEO of the hospital?

• Is the most talented and creative engineer or scientist the right person to be the vice president of research and development?

• Should the most engaging and liveliest professor on campus be a considered a future university president?

• Is the best marksman and the strongest, fastest soldier going to make the best general?

Maybe. But all too often, maybe not.

The Reluctant Leader: Myth and Reality

In novels, TV shows, movies, and even the real world, there are plenty of examples of "reluctant leaders." I'm talking about those who didn't seek out responsibility and probably didn't want it, but had it imposed on them and were successful at it.

However, on balance, good leaders *want* to be in charge, and are willing to work hard to develop the abilities needed to succeed in this very unique role. I don't want the preceding paragraphs to come across as discouraging to aspiring leaders. In fact, I would rarely discourage a capable, dedicated individual from pursuing a leadership job. I just think it's important to know that it's what they truly want and that they want it for the right reasons.

To give you a quick example from own career, when I was a captain, I found myself feeling a pretty big void in my life. I wasn't as happy or fulfilled in the Army as I'd been in the past. For years, I had returned home from my morning Army physical fitness session all fired up and excited. I would charge through the house exclaiming "Good PT! Good PT!" My children thought I was nuts because I would get so enthusiastic just because of the physical exercise. (For those who didn't grow up in a military family, it has its own special joys and memories, like having your dad run around the house saying crazy things like this.)

However, my motivation began to wane to the point that I told my wife I was considering leaving the Army after 16 years (and after being recently selected for early promotion to major), which was just four years short of earning a retirement. It is extremely rare for a soldier to even think about resigning at that point in their service.

I couldn't put my finger on it, but I had just plain lost my passion for the military. My wife told me I really needed to think about what I was doing and not to worry that we had invested those 16 years of our lives serving the Army. If I didn't want to stay, we'd find another path to follow. (What a great lady!) I did exactly what she advised. I gave it a great deal of thought and soul-searching. And an old memory hit me right between my eyes.

So, as a young captain and Army leader, I asked myself several of the questions mentioned above. Including, did I really want to be a leader? And the truth is, I was able to answer yes to most all of them—enthusiastically and passionately.

It became clear to me that my real purpose—my "positive motivator"—was that I wanted to lead and to serve alongside the soldiers and organization I was so proud to be with. I loved soldiers and the kinds of people who were in the Army. I enjoyed building and being a part of teams. And I enjoyed laying out goals and helping others achieve them.

I even enjoyed resolving conflicts and turning tough debates and seemingly intractable arguments into mutual understanding, productive compromise, and a shared "way ahead." In fact, after taking a pretty hard look at myself, I realized that helping make the soldiers around me was all that I really wanted to do with my days in the Army. I relished looking young sergeants and lieutenants in the eye, and after giving them a tough mission, seeing them look right back at me and say, *"I got this, sir,"* and feeling like I had helped give them that confidence.

In short, after some serious thought about whether I wanted to lead, I decided to stay in the Army. And this might sound like I'm making it up, but after that, I didn't have a single truly bad day *(okay, maybe one or two)*. Every day wasn't easy, but I knew my purpose and enjoyed the responsibilities the Army entrusted me with. And I'm glad I had the chance at one point to question the path I was on and to think seriously about what I was best suited to do. Everyone should engage in the same kind of soul-searching, before your career lands you somewhere you don't want to be.

CHAPTER 12:

LIKE A DUCK
(Look Smooth – Paddle Hard)

As a leader, I found that perfectionism is one of the toughest instincts to overcome. It can sometimes be a cover for fear. Fear of failure *(even minor ones)*; fear of looking bad *(especially in front of your boss or your troops)*; fear of missing a detail or two; fear of losing control. Perfectionism born of fear stifles innovation, instills a rigid adherence to appearance over substance, and undermines the creativity and initiative we want in our team members.

Learning to recognize when you're driven by fear—and then stopping that fear in its tracks—is a fundamental leadership skill. Though perfectionism driven by fear should be avoided, *striving for perfection*—while recognizing you will never reach it—is a great way to achieve excellence. If you set your standards high, even when you miss the mark by a little, you'll still likely obtain excellent results.

High Standards and Consistency Are Crucial

My first ten years in the Army, I struggled with understanding the difference between competing against other people and reaching high standards. Like many people, I focused my attention on competing against others and always wanting to do better. I suppose that's human nature. Prior to taking a physical fitness test, I would agonize the night before to the point I couldn't sleep *(which did not help my performance)*. To even think that someone would score higher than me would make me sick to my stomach. But what I've learned over the years is that you're not going to be number one at everything. And the sooner you accept that, the faster you'll grow as a leader.

Whenever possible, compete against the standard you want to reach, not against your teammates. Knowing that you have done your best with your God-given talents will help you sleep a lot better at night.

Good leaders not only set high standards and enforce them, they use others as a bench mark to better themselves and their organizations. They don't apologize for maintaining high standards and don't hesitate to point out when they haven't been met.

In the military, standards are often set on an individual and a unit basis. Individual standards are based on a number of known guidelines, so that soldiers and their leaders have an ongoing measure of their performance. For soldiers, everything from physical fitness to marksmanship to appearance in uniform is tested. At any given moment, each soldier knows where they excel and where they need to improve—and so does their commander.

Unit standards are established so commands have specific performance measurements to guide their training and which set objectives connected to the unit's mission. It's the responsibility of military leaders to make sure that these objectives are understood by everyone and that they have the resources—and motivation— to achieve these goals. Good leaders do this through constant communication and by setting the highest example of personal discipline and commitment.

As a young company commander on the Trans-Korea Petroleum Pipeline, responsible for providing petroleum to soldiers all across the northern region of South Korea, I didn't always understand this. Luckily, the Army has various kinds of competitions among units. They channel the competitive instincts of many soldiers and leaders in ways that encourage esprit de corps while ensuring that units are evaluated on the standards and tasks they'll have to perform in a combat deployment. A number of these competitions focus on units that perform supply, maintenance, and logistics missions. When my battalion commander in Korea informed his company commanders that our units would compete in one of these competitions, I thought this was a waste of time given all of our other responsibilities and that it would keep my soldiers from performing more urgent tasks.

However, in the Army, orders are orders. And as we prepared my company for the competition, I realized not only how demanding and high the standards were for winning, but that the Army had done a pretty good job of making sure the tasks we'd perform to win the competition corresponded to the tasks we'd perform in wartime. Our unit's soldiers could see that the competition was worth their effort. If a soldier received one of these awards, it confirmed that they were among the best of the best.

Well, despite my initial skepticism, and due to the work of the non-commissioned officers and soldiers in my company, we won the Army Maintenance Excellence Award. Which meant we were the best company-level maintenance unit in the entire Army. We then went on to represent the Army in the Department of Defense–level competition. Competing in both of these competitions had a remarkable effect on our unit; we grew as a team, both personally and professionally. Creating a climate that rewards meeting the highest standards, while providing opportunities to hone healthy competitive instincts, makes both the individual and organization better.

The Importance of Competence and Hard Work

Sometimes it's the obvious that gets overlooked. While it might be self-evident, good leaders must be competent at the tasks they're assigned, and they must demonstrate it. There are few things that undermine a leader, especially a new leader, faster than signaling to their troops, employees, peers, and bosses that they don't know what they're doing. In a strong organization with dedicated employees, people will put up with a lot from their leaders—everything from short deadlines to long meetings to the personality quirks that we all have. But they seldom put up with incompetence, at least for very long.

Does that mean you have to know more than anyone else in your office, section, or unit? Or that you are never allowed to make a mistake? No, of course, on both counts.

Most often, people define "competence" in their leaders as a mixture of the following behaviors:

- Demonstrating sound, reasonable judgment
- Providing understandable and actionable guidance
- Willing to listen *(really listen)* to experts who have more knowledge
- Making decisions that *(even when others do not agree with them)* are justifiable and communicated clearly
- Setting reasonable expectations, goals, and deadlines
- Providing prompt, constructive feedback on individual and group performance
- Always treating people with respect—especially when delivering criticism and resolving conflicts. (You get bonus points if you can do this when you're tired, irritable, and feeling overwhelmed yourself.)

The fact of the matter is that becoming and remaining a good leader is more often a product of sheer hard work than anything else. Like incompetence, a hint of laziness or a lack of diligence in the execution of a leader's duties is corrosive of an organization's effectiveness. Put simply, once you're a leader, you are going to have to work your butt off. Admit it, you asked for this. That means putting in the time and effort to read and learn everything you can about your section, unit, or organization—its policies, procedures, regulations, goals, missions, and the measures by which your success is determined. You also need to learn about your competition (in the armed forces, that means "the enemy"). Again, you don't have to be as knowledgeable as the most experienced subject-matter experts you lead, but you do need to understand where your ignorance resides, and then take active steps to fix it.

Like a Duck

Leaders are often compared (and compare themselves) to animals. Usually animals like lions, tigers, sharks, eagles, and hawks. Sometimes leaders are as fast as cheetahs; other times they're wise as owls. Or they might be the "800-pound gorilla" or the "elephant in the room."

I would like to nominate a different animal for the aspiring leader to compare themselves to: the humble duck.

Not very heroic or intimidating, I admit. However, when you really think for a minute about all that ducks can do, they're a good choice.

For example, ducks are expert navigators. Without the aid of satellites, GPS, or even an old-fashioned paper map, the average, run-of-the-mill duck can find its way from New England to South Carolina (a distance of about 1,100 miles) and back again every year. They do it while making sure that members of their flock all start and end the journey together, while stopping daily along the way for food, rest, and fuel. Pretty impressive leadership and teamwork when you think about it.

Moreover, when a duck finally arrives at their destination, normally a lake or pond, after all that exhausting effort, they're usually calmly gliding across the top of the water looking relaxed, rested and ready to do it all over again. Again, a mighty good example of the traits you need as a leader.

As most of us know, even when the duck is moving across the water, what they're really doing is paddling like the dickens underneath. Whenever you're paddling hardest under the water, that's when it's most important to appear smooth as a duck to everyone who can see you. It's what good leaders do.

I learned the importance of acting calm as a duck about six months after I was commissioned to second lieutenant. My first assignment as an Army officer was with the 887th Supply Detachment in South Texas in the small town of Alice. It was a small detachment which consisted of approximately 60 soldiers. One day during lunch, my platoon leader (we both were lieutenants) come running into my office to tell me she was being harassed by a soldier. The soldier stood about six feet tall with very broad shoulders; he weighed about 210 pounds. I asked the first sergeant to bring the soldier into my office at 1300 hours (1 P.M.) along with the platoon leader. Once the soldier reported to me, I began to ask him questions. It quickly became apparent that the soldier was intoxicated. When I asked him my second question, he placed both of his hands on my desk, leaned over, looked at me menacingly, and snarled, "I am going to bash your head, nigger." My initial thought was to jump across my desk and see who was the better man with his fists. But, I knew good leaders think before reacting and control their emotions. I can honestly say I appeared calm as a duck *(but I was seething underneath)*. Three months later, that Soldier was discharged from the Army Reserve.

Even if we're not being threatened with violence, the fact is we all get frustrated. However, those who've been entrusted with the privilege of command lose the right to let that frustration show. This doesn't mean that great leaders never show emotion. They do. It just means that great leaders are deliberate and purposeful when expressing their emotions. When you believe your troops need to see the boss "get mad," then "get mad," but do it with intent and knowing that, on the inside, you remain in control. As Thomas Jefferson once said, *"Nothing gives one man so great an advantage over another as to remain calm in all circumstances."*

As military leaders, we train and prepare for combat all our lives. It's in combat that we prove our worth, both to those we lead and to the nation we defend. It is therefore of the highest importance that we learn to discipline our emotions—like we discipline our bodies—to overcome the stresses of war. Corporate leaders also have to control their emotions, or they might not be leaders for long.

Handling Punches in the Gut

When I was serving as the commanding general of CASCOM in Fort Lee, Virginia, we had three motorcycle accidents that resulted in four tragic deaths—all in one year. Any time you lose a soldier, family member, or employee, you should be asking yourself what could have been done to prevent it. After a great deal of brainstorming with our staff, we concluded that we were doing lots of things right when it came to ensuring the safety of our soldiers. However, we also realized there was room for improvement, and we worked hard to address shortcomings in our motorcycle safety program. When you lead large military commands with thousands of soldiers and civilian employees, painful tragedies occur. But you have to do everything possible to prevent them.

I met with the families and spouses of those who had died in the motorcycle accidents. I offered support and did whatever I could to help them. I also talked to my boss, General Bob Cone, about the accidents. He had been through even more difficult times. General Cone had been the commanding general at Fort Hood, Texas, in November 2009 when Nidal Malik Hasan, a U.S. Army major and psychiatrist, killed 13 people and injured more than 30 others in the infamous mass shooting there. It was the worst mass murder at a U.S. military base in history. Hasan opened fire at a processing center where soldiers were getting medical check-ups before heading overseas or returning from a deployment.

How you handle the aftermath of such incidents matters a lot. But you can do all the right things, and they are still devastating;

they will feel like a punch in the gut. You have to confront tragedies head-on, overcome them, and help those around you navigate
through them. Tragedies like the motorcycle accidents, and particularly the Hasan shootings, are the ultimate tests of leadership and
integrity. You can do everything else right in your job, but you'll be
judged by how you handle yourself when the worst happens.

The Mirror Test

Over the course of a lifetime, by some estimates we spend more
than two years looking at ourselves in the mirror. More than two
years—shaving, brushing our teeth, combing our hair, or just
preening or scrutinizing or worrying about our appearance. In the
morning, in the evening, and at other times during the day, we may
also steal a glance at our reflection in a window while walking past
an office building. Even the humblest among us spend a lot of time
just flat-out staring at ourselves.

Human beings are some of the only animals able to recognize
themselves in the mirror, and they take full advantage of it. Those
who study the behavior and psychology of animals sometimes use
the "mirror test" to gauge the level of self-awareness of different animal species. Chimpanzees can recognize themselves, so can gorillas
and dolphins. Dogs, unfortunately, cannot. (As a dog lover, I'm not
totally convinced of that, and I assume the scientists never met our
Pomeranian, *Dallas*.)

The self-awareness that allows human beings to recognize themselves in the mirror is actually an important trait when it comes to leadership. In many respects, truly candid and relentlessly honest self-awareness is the foundation of genuine leadership. Yet it is all too rarely practiced.

The most effective leaders have often made a kind of study of themselves. Not because they are egocentric, self-centered, or vain. On the contrary, gifted leaders pursue self-awareness because they understand how critical it is to know one's own strengths, weaknesses, talents, and flaws. Good leaders are constantly on the lookout for the triggers likely to render them short-tempered, irritable, unduly critical, unreceptive to new ideas, or simply lacking in basic courtesy.

Self-awareness of one's capacities and limitations, as uncomfortable as it can be, is a pivotal step to becoming a good leader. Leadership requires an almost Buddhist-like "mindfulness" of how our thoughts work and how they affect the way we relate to those around us.

For someone who aspires to lead others, the "mirror test" is about a lot more than getting a clean shave or covering up those gray hairs. For leaders, those moments spent in front of the mirror—in the morning and the evening especially—are an absolutely critical time to deepen your self-awareness, prepare for a new day, or review what happened in the day that just ended.

When self-aware leaders look at the mirror first thing in the morning, they know it's an opportunity to ask themselves some necessary and often tough questions:

✓ Who am I meeting with today?

✓ What are their goals, interests, and objectives?

✓ If I have worked with them before, how will their personality traits affect what we need to accomplish together?

✓ Are they quick to anger? Defensive? Shy? Aggressive? If I am senior to them? Will they simply defer to whatever I say, or will they engage in discussion and challenge my assertions?

✓ What are my own objectives for today?

✓ Who should I listen to today? Whose advice should I seek out?

✓ What do I want to have accomplished when I look back in this same mirror tonight?

✓ Finally, would I want to work for me?

Like every mission, good leadership takes planning and forethought. Letting it just "happen" is a recipe for failure. Spending a few moments in front of the mirror in the morning and thinking through, even rehearsing, how you will handle the leadership challenges of the coming day is a great method for approaching events with confidence and recognizing the hurdles you will need to surmount so that you don't run right into them. Prepare yourself—mentally, physically, and spiritually—at the start of each and every day.

Similarly, at the end of the day, when you're standing there brushing your teeth before going to bed, is a perfect moment to reflect on how you did, again by asking yourself tough questions and having the self-awareness to answer them honestly:

✓ What could have gone better today?

✓ How could I have handled that meeting, conversation, or counseling session better so that our individual and organizational goals would have been met?

✓ Did I help inspire, mentor, coach, or simply lend a compassionate ear to someone else today?

✓ Did I really give it my best today, or did I hold something back? If so, why?

I am not suggesting that developing the skills of a good leader requires that you constantly second-guess yourself. That's not what the "mirror test" is about. You are going to make mistakes. You will be criticized. Not everyone will agree with you. Not everyone will even like you. Recognize all that, treat everyone with professionalism and respect, and work hard to get over those daily mistakes that are part of everyone's life.

The "mirror test" is about developing daily habits that build your self-awareness and, when combined with courage, determination, integrity, and candor, will make you a better leader and a better person (these two things are not mutually exclusive). After all, if you're going to spend two whole years of your life looking at yourself, you might as well make the most of it!

Takeaways:

* Ask yourself whether you truly want to be a leader
* Excellence does not occur by accident
* Compete against the standards of your organization, not against your teammates
* Discipline your emotions
* Ask yourself, "Would I want to work for me?"

AFTERWORD
(*The Future from my Foxhole*)

The U.S. Army will continue to operate in an environment marked by considerable political, economic, and military competition and rapidly evolving threats in the years ahead. Adversaries will employ innovative tactics and advanced technologies. Opponents will include conventional military forces (both state and non-state), unconventional forces such as irregular militias and paramilitaries, terrorists, and even criminals. They may have access to "standoff weapons" (i.e., longer-range weapons that allow for evading return fire) and other modern weaponry, including those capable of mass destruction. Some opponents will emerge almost spontaneously in response to U.S. actions overseas. Many will have the capacity to wage protracted wars.

Some adversaries will avoid fighting conventional U.S. forces directly and attempt to exploit perceived U.S. weaknesses. They will see the heavy yet essential U.S. reliance on seaports and airfields as staging areas as vulnerabilities. Communications, fuel supplies, sustainment convoys, and other surface movements will also be targeted. And, through expanding Anti-Access/Area-Denial mechanisms, they will try to deny U.S. access to theaters of operations across the globe. Army units must be able to move rapidly, minimize our vulnerability to electromagnetic spectrum threats, evade long-range precision fires, employ unmanned ground and aviation systems – all while locating, closing with and destroying enemy forces. We'll have to do this with a flexible, logistics footprint that sustains our troops – while contributing to their speed and lethality. The days of large, semi-permanent, forward operating bases, particularly in a fight against a peer competitor, are likely over.

Even with the increased threat posed by major state actors, non-state and unconventional adversarial forces will still present tremendous challenges. The U.S. response to them is blurring the distinction between military operations and law enforcement. Providing security to civilians in areas where they're active requires that the U.S. Army conduct a gamut of logistics and life-support operations.

The U.S. homeland also remains vulnerable to attacks from terrorists. While al-Qaeda and affiliated groups have been weakened, terrorists will likely attempt to strike the homeland in the future Moreover, they will continue to recruit members while attracting sympathizers; religious fervor will not be their only impulse, as many oppose the U.S. presence in their regions on political grounds as well.

Although our technological edge may be eroding in relation to peer competitors like China and Russia in specific areas, overall U.S. technological progress will continue to enhance our ability to contend with these threats to national security. Advances in artificial intelligence, data science, robotic systems, geo-spatial intelligence, biotechnology and nanotechnology will contribute to many key military, logistics breakthroughs, in information technology, sensor and network technology, and energy storage and transfer. Yet, adversaries with sufficient financial resources will also adopt these emerging technologies.

As my former boss General Dave Perkins would often remark, the future is "unknown and unknowable."

Change is a certainty. Rapid change. And if you do not change with it, you will find yourself behind the eight ball.

Just as the Army has to plan to sustain itself in the next war, corporations need to prepare the way for their sustainment operations down the road. They must discern key patterns and trends in the world around them to manage their supply chains effectively. They must have a supply chain strategy that stretches years ahead. And, like the Army, they must be agile, adaptive, and able to adjust to evolving circumstances.

Some recent trends in supply chain management include use of robots in warehouses, expense-cutting and optimization driven by rising shipping costs, use of cloud-based software, distribution of inventory to more warehouses, employment of stronger cyber-security measures, utilization of artificial intelligence and supply planning digital transformation.[18]

All logisticians must put their customers first. That's as axiomatic in the military as in business. As I wrote at the top of this book, logisticians are professional "givers." They focus on providing

18   https://selecthub.com/supply-chain-management/supply-chain-management-future-trends/.

to someone else. In the private sector, that means satisfying the needs of people who buy their products and services. In the military, it means making sure that warfighters have what they need. Although technology is driving a genuine revolution across the logistics and supply-chain fields, the ethos of our profession will remain the same. Logisticians must deliver. We must be willing "to give the shirts off our backs and boots off our feet."

Nothing less will do.

After 42 years, my retirement ceremony and farewell with General Perna, June 2017 at Redstone Arsenal, Alabama

Two important aspects of Army life are friendships and transitions. Soldiers are continually transitioning from one unit to another all across the globe. The friendships you make throughout those transitions sustain you over time. As I made my final transition out of the Army, a close friend and great logistician, General Gus Perna, presided at my retirement ceremony. Gus and I have known each other for years. General Perna commanded the U.S. Army Materiel Command and was the right leader at the right time for that organization. I was fortunate to have the chance to serve as his Deputy and consider him the model for Army logisticians and leaders everywhere.

CPSIA information can be obtained
at www.ICGtesting.com
Printed in the USA
FSHW021559051119

9 781949 758368